DISCLAIMER

This is a fiction. Names, Characters, Business, Events and Incidents are the author's imagination. Any resemblance to any persons, living or dead or actual events or localities is purely coincidental.

KASTURI

The musk in you

ANAMIKA S YADAV

First Published in November 2022

ISBN: 978-93-5680-342-8

Cover Design:
Anuj Yadav

ACKNOWLEDGMENTS

This book wouldn't have been possible without the moral support of My Family and Friends.

Special thanks to Udaykumar sir for his valuable guidance.

Can't thank enough to my dearest friend Leena for accompanying me throughout this journey of Kasturi.

Love to my dear Shaurya and Tisya who gave reason to write yet another Novel.

DEDICATION

I dedicate this book to my Aai (Mother) who has always been a living example for never giving up and standing strong always.

"With the smell etched in her soul, the musk deer galloped through strangers, searching for her own."

You are about to read a story (the book is a work of fiction) about the travails of a woman who is a simple happy girl, with a zest for life and had a dream to build and succeed in her business ventures, balancing this with her duties on the personal front.

'Kasturi' is not just the name of a woman. It is the inner alluring fragrance that a musk deer carries within itself but searches everywhere outside its own body to find the source. The protagonist of this book goes through a painful but illuminating journey to discover that search.

Now, read her exciting story.

SK

ओझं होतं ते माझं
कणाकणाने साठलेलं
मीच माझ्या वाटेवरती
नकळत कधी गाठलेलं...

हृदयात गर्दी भारी
भावनांच्या प्रवासाची
काहि जाणता तर
अजाणता भेटल्या काही...

पाउलखुणा सोबतीच्या
वाटलेल्या ओळखीच्या
मोह पडता संगतीचा
अनोळखी भासे त्याही...

प्रतिबिंब पाण्यातील ते
माझेच वाटलेले
कितीच वादळे पण
गुंफुन साठलेले....

...Ana

10

KASTURI

The musk in you

The baggage I carried belonged to me, which I unknowingly gathered bit by bit as I walked my way.

Heart is full of entangled emotions met knowingly and unknowingly.

Footsteps which accompanied and were thought to be known appeared to be unknown as I got used to the company.

The reflection in the water looked to be mine. It is made of many storms stringed together.

Here is a story of Kasturi.

"Who is she?"

She is just another lady. Maybe sitting next to you on the 4th seat of a fast local train, a lady standing in a queue behind you to take a ferry to her destination, a lady staying next door whose voice may not be soothing but sings regularly as she cooks.

Some days she is a mess, some days she is a fighter and knowingly or unknowingly some days she is a bit of both as the situation demands. But every moment she is there facing, fighting, trying but never giving up.

Contents

The Beginning

Travelling was not only her requirement due to the nature of her business but also her hobby, her passion. While Kasturi travelled 7-8hrs for a meeting of just 20-25mins the rest of the day she would visit temples, markets, villages, and farms. It didn't bother her if it was a sunny, windy, or rainy day. She was always on her wheels as her mom describes her.

It was not accidental but Kasturi has been talking to this community at Vivekwadi since the couple of times she visited this place. Their art of making utility, decorative items, and attractive showpieces out of bamboo drove her crazy. This place was close to the hospital she visited.

Kashi always stared at her while Kasturi sat and had Jhunka-Bhakri at this small restaurant whenever she visited this place. This afternoon Kasturi orders the same along with a glass of buttermilk. Tiny Kashi runs towards her, hands over a beautifully carved pen holder, and runs back to her place. She is standing, staring at Kasturi from behind her grandfather. Kashi's cute smile pleases Kasturi. She gets curious looking at the handmade craft item out of a bamboo piece. This initiates talk between Kasturi and Kashi's grandfather. On subsequent visits, Kasturi meets many such small-scale workers making and selling such articles in the local market. She speaks to them and forms a small firm where these villagers made such articles and 'Femys Creations' would export these to African countries where Kasturi's existing business already had base and contacts. 'Femys creations' picked up well and Kasturi was happy to share the margins with the craftsman. From five to fifty, workers and their families were happy to be part of Femys. Within two years, it reached a satisfactory level.

While Kasturi's better half Avinash was not convinced about this business, still was a strong support for her. Growth demanded complete-time, dedication and more funds. Sheela, Kasturi's close friend was given charge at the Vivekwadi warehouse where all these articles would be stored and transported to destinations every quarter. It was not difficult to arrange funds as many of her known people witnessed the growth of Femys and willingly invested. Kasturi's investment made the larger portion though.

Sheela was single, trying to come to terms after she broke up her live-in relationship of more than 2years. Her relationship had broken all the ties with her parents as well. Kasturi had no second thought about handing over Femys to her and she too needed such an opportunity.

That was just when she thought everything was going right. Kids were growing, Parents and In-laws were healthy and all was well between siblings. Happy and well-satisfied marriage, small but steady and consistent business, and cherry on the icing was 'Femys creation'. Being associated with the craftsmen in rural territory gave Kasturi a different level of satisfaction and a feeling of accomplishment. Sheela took over the business very confidently and was a decision-maker in no time. She practically took over the business completely and Kasturi was able to devote full time to her existing business. Everything was smooth and sorted. What else could anyone ask for?

Staring out of a small window of her unventilated flat, she wondered looking at the bungalow at a distance which always caught her sight, and she recollects many of her friend's words "enough of this small house now, kids are growing and we are almost 40. If not now when are you planning to buy a bigger house?"

She always had a thought which flashed several times as if she said to herself "when we buy another house everyone will wonder, it was worth waiting for." She feels why this statement flashes always and she just smiles.

Standing at the window thinking all about her life her mind picks another statement from some movie, "My life is so plain, please make it a bit interesting dear God" she again smiles at herself, turns around and the routine continues.

Probably God takes it too seriously. Read it for your self how much spice was then added to her so-called plain dal-rice with pure ghee topping type life. Read it for yourself and taste a bit; if the spice was fair enough?

KASTURI

On this day of early monsoon, Kasturi is sitting on the extension of one of the windows of the same bungalow she always looked at; gazing at her old house, now from the other side. Early in the morning, the air is cool and moist. Some storms passing through nearby states result in windy weather. It is been months since she has tried to restart her yoga and failed to do so. Uncontrollable rough hairs and flapped tummy give her a not-so-good feeling.

Looking at the flyover and the vehicles passing by, she recollects what makes her heartbeat sink deep and deep.

Few years back while passing over one such flyover in Mumbai and sitting on the back seat of a bike a thought dashed, "what if I lose all my money suddenly." She shook her head, "what am I thinking?"

Why did this come to my mind then?

Her eyes are deserted and what surrounds are only dark circles. Inside she weeps, she wants to shout and cry aloud to vent but holds the storm and stops herself from breaking down as she can't afford it until she fulfils her commitments.

Her journey, from 6th floor unventilated flat to the breezy one she Rajfested unknowingly, her journey from 'her eyes full of hope and confidence to the deserted dark circled' is just another word for a roller coaster ride and now, she has decided to jump out of it with no idea where she will land.

Where exactly did things go wrong? Which decision was first to fall out of place? Which blow brought down her castle? Or the castle still exists and needs to know if it falls into pieces or she is able to rebuild its strength?

At the age of mid-40, she is burdened with heavy loans whose monthly EMIs not only break her finances bit by bit but also her hope bit by bit and her confidence bit by bit. Each time she gathers her bits herself and stands trying to be strong.

Kasturi is trying to figure out Varun in the garden and suddenly she notices a group of kids running to overtake one another. All stopping at the cycle shop and taking out a rupee note, all of them offer it to the shopkeeper who rents the cycle for one hour. Everyone had their pick and this tiny little girl is struggling to hold the cycle. Her friends flew with their cycle and this girl could ride it only when the shopkeeper helped her. He holds her cycle from behind till she tries to takes a pace. Trying to balance but she is not able to control it as usual. She paddles hard while the shopkeeper laughs from behind saying, "be confident else you won't be able to do it ever."

She is not able to manage her confidence and screams "move asiiiiiide" before dashing with a milkman. Milk spills over and spreads all over the road. Before the milkman could get up, her friends come to her rescue and run dragging the girl and her bicycle to save both from the anger of the milkman.

All of them run out of this garden while the tiny little girl looks back up at Kasturi. She is not able to understand what she was witnessing in front of her. It is Kasturi herself looking at her grown-up version. She comes to the present moment with the loud voice of Varun saying, "mamma, here" waving his hand at her while riding the bicycle.

Years passed to this incident but it always appears and reappears in front of her. Deep down she wants to get rid of her fear but could never.

Once a fearful little girl is now fighting on many fronts, standing strong and unbroken just like the strong, aged tree whose leaves are dropped due to rough seasons but still, its strength flaunts, flaunts as the roots are deep and strong.

Paving the wrong road

She puts both her kids to sleep and is just about to put her phone on flight mode before going to bed. Holding it in her hand, she walks down to pick up a water jar and suddenly her phone vibrates in her hand. She looks at the screen, flipping the right side of the phone towards herself, and tries to focus on the name displayed, "Manav!" she exclaims! She looks at the wall clock and murmurs, "why is he calling at this hour?" It is already 10.45pm. The other side says, "hi, sleeping?" as soon as she receives the call. She responds, "Yes just about to." How come calling so late?"

Manav begins, and she becomes restless. Her face searches for expressions, her heartbeat pace to survive. She continues to listen to him as she slowly climbs the stairs running from the living room to her bedroom, moving at an erratic pace. She finds herself too heavy to carry any further and simply slides down resting on the wall, holding the railing, and resting herself on one of the stairs.

Manav asks, "Who is Sheela? What is Femys Creations?" How are you involved? "She responds, "My friend, and I have only my capital invested currently."

She is numb while listening to what Manav is saying from the other side. She is also surprised and perplexed as to how and why he is aware of this. Manav continues limiting her to speak. He pours lots of information and she manages to interrupt in between, "how do you know all this?"

Manav is blunt. "How do I know is not your worry? Worry about your finances and don't worry about the authenticity of my information; it is true." He continues, "Your CA, your so-called friend has hidden lots of information from you which is more than anyone can cheat, and your husband, your family won't trust you anymore."

She is shaking, her heart breaking as she shifts her handset from left to right ear. Her left ear is practically more than warm by now. She rests her head back on the wall as Manav continues to add "you need to calm down. I am there for you and your family. You just need to make certain decisions and I will help you come out of this crisis."

She listens but doesn't want to believe what he says. "My earnings are coming regularly and so do other investor's. Sheela never mentioned it and she doesn't hide anything from me." Manav cuts in between "come to reality, you will not receive anything after a couple of months so don't waste your time on sentiments. Only I can save you and we need at least Rs.10-12 lacs to spend to get this work done. Your company is sinking and we will try to get it covered under 'sick unit', get some funds from some Government scheme and try to retrieve it." She doesn't completely believe what he says, but the details match with her knowledge so she finds it difficult to dispel.

 He tries to console, "don't go cross-verifying my information, it will only give you more pain. Just organise the amount and call me. I will take care of everything." Before she could respond to him he continues "don't tell anyone about it. Not your friend, not even your husband. We will manage and come out of the crisis."

She quietly replies, "how is that possible, Manav? Where will I get Rs.12 lacs from? We have invested everything we had in this business and complications with this new house have further drained our finances. Firstly, I won't hide this from both of them secondly; I can't arrange funds myself."

Manav reacts with a slightly annoyed tone, "ok, do whatever you want" then calms down a bit saying, "whatever you can organise do it and call me, the rest I will take care of" and he hangs up saying "good night."

She looks at the home screen of her cell phone. He has been talking for almost an hour.

Few days back Manav was supposed to meet her in Kolhapur to help finalise a big order. He made her wait and wait for two days and didn't turn up. When it was time for her train she received a message from him "shall meet you tomorrow in Mumbai." He arrived in Mumbai, called Kasturi but didn't meet and then went absconding for days.

And what was he doing? Suddenly calling at this odd hour after so many days mentioning all this; whatever Manav mentions is too scary. Her family members and their investments run through her thoughts in a flash. She continues to sit in that place unable to move or think rationally.

She wondered why Manav didn't want me to talk about this with anyone. With the slight hope that this is all not correct, she immediately calls Sudesh her CA. Sudesh is working for and looking after Femys in close coordination with Sheela for any financial transactions.

"Hi, I am sorry for calling you so late, but…" Sudesh, as expected, sounds sleepy. He replies "no problem but at midnight? What happened? Is everything fine?" She counter questions "you need to tell me if everything is fine, Sudesh?" He is clueless. "What is it? What are you asking about?" Sudesh questions her. She continues "there is this person from Kolhapur known to me who had called and mentioned some details about Femys Creations." She briefs what she heard from Manav. Sudesh initially responds with "hmm, true" and later stops even using that expression. He is more shocked than her. She checks "Sudesh, are you there?" "Yes, very much; who is this person and how does he know all this?" he too is surprised.

She is anxious to know the other part, "Sudesh, is Femys under financial crisis? Did you guys hide something from me that you were not supposed to?

Is the company sinking? Are we having a problem?" She continues with absolutely no response from the other side. She yells "are you there? Are you going to respond?"

"To my surprise, whatever he mentioned is correct. All details are correct. I am surprised. How come someone knows these details about our firm? Who is he?" Her voice sinks. She interrupts "are we in a mess? Is the company in crisis?" Her heart would have burst, but for the constant flow of tears down her cheeks. She is not able to utter a word, and there is silence from either side as Sudesh confirms Manav's details again. Slowly, Sudesh whispers "hello" and she replies, "give me two minutes, i shall call back." She disconnects and before another moment dials again. Swallowing her congestion she briefs "this person says there is some Government scheme under which sick units are given funds to recover and then they have to be repaid in some years, and these funds are at low-interest rates, and that he will help us to get this facility, and we can save the worst. But we need to pay him around Rs.12 lacs for this and where will this money come from? I don't know what is to be done. I don't know how to tell this to everyone, and Avinash is sleeping, and how will everybody respond?" Sudesh, are you sure this is true? "He again responds, "Yes, and if this person can help you, please take his help." "Where do I get this money from? I have put everything I had and everything I didn't have into Femys Creations."

Sudesh makes an unsuccessful attempt to console her,

"If at all someone can arrange this amount, it is only you." She breaks down. You don't understand Sudesh, this person has a liking for me and I don't know if he has some hidden agenda in finding all these details and trying to help. Sudesh explains, "the financial crisis is huge." She asks "What amount are we in the negative?" There is silence from the other side, her voice rising again before she hears "around 5 crores'." This was the exact amount mentioned by Manav and this keeps resonating. She hangs up saying "Sudesh, you could have mentioned all this to me?"

She rushes to her room without giving herself time to think if she should mention it to her husband. Sitting on the floor and rubbing her palm on his back, she tries to wake him up. "Get up, there is a serious problem." After understanding that he is not minding what she is trying to say, she directly mentions "Listen, Femys Creations is sinking into very heavy losses." Our money is gone, and she bursts into tears. He still doesn't bother to get up. Just lying in his position he says "I know that, let's talk in the morning." This surprises her even more; "how is it that you are aware of this? She continues, "You are not getting me. It is not a small sum; the loss is estimated to be in crores. He raises his head as she gets up, standing straight in front of him. She further mentions, "Manav just called and mentioned what Sheela or Sudesh would have told us much earlier. I don't know why though. I cross verified it with Sudesh, he confirms that is correct." He stares at her for a couple of seconds and goes back to sleep saying, "it can be discussed in the morning."

But, how could she sleep?

Her mind, her heart, her family, and her world is about to be grabbed by the worst storm.

She has been standing in one position for a long time, she didn't realise for how long. Suddenly, she is gasping for breath, which moves her. She runs out onto the terrace and keeps walking from one wall to another trying to calm herself. Her husband, her parents, her siblings, and her kids, all those from Vivekwadi are there looking at her, ready with questions and shouting aloud at her. She looks up at the open sky, stretching her arms towards the sky and questioning why? Why did this happen? How? She collapses down, scratching the floor and getting wild on herself.

She drops herself on the floor. She wants to scream but just closes her eyes. She dials Sheela's number but disconnects before it gets connected. All those words of Manav and Sudesh run through continuously and then she is scared to close her eyes. She weeps biting the corner of her palm and feels drowsy after some time. Her eyelids droop but she is not able to sleep. She wish she could just get up in the morning and find that everything was normal and whatever she heard on the phone was nothing more than a nightmare. In her half-consciousness she whispers lots which no one witnesses, not even she is aware of what she murmurs through the night.

Early in the morning, she tries to open her heavy eyelids. It is peak winter and her body is almost numb by this time. She struggles to get up and move her limbs slowly one at a time and then the rest of her body until she manages to sit dragging her body back and resting her back on the terrace wall.

It is still dark outside. She gets up with difficulty and sits down beside Avinash. Avinash feels her touch and gets up "I learnt this a few days back, but I was just waiting if Sheela comes to us and reveals. I didn't want you to know this from me." Kasturi is in uncontrolled tears while Avinash just leaves as he has nothing more to say. She wants to again repeat what Manav proposed but Avinash is in no mood to talk about anything right now. Not knowing what next, Kasturi gets back to her daily routine; her mind and soul are shaken.

She informs Avinash that she will only make a few phone calls from home today and will not be joining him at the office. He picks up his lunch box and leaves before Kasturi can bring up the subject again. The whole of the day Kasturi spends like a nightmare putting all the figures on paper, writing the names of those who all invested on her say. There is a dark cloud in front of her and a small hope torched by Manav.

Days pass and Avinash is not willing to talk about this matter till Kasturi makes him sit forcefully and narrates all about the call from Manav, followed by her call to Sudesh in detail. "It is not going to be easy. We don't have money to gamble on what this person is proposing" Avinash utters, "Yes I know, but if there is any such option as he says, we can try and explore it from some other source" Kasturi suggests.

After quite a bit of discussion, they decide to reach out to their family friend Dr.Rathi, their business associate from Latur who also happens to be politically well connected. He has high regard for both of them.Until now, neither of them had mentioned anything to Sheela and she too is unaware that they knew anything about the whole matter. Monthly amounts are still regular from Sheela.

Kasturi speaks to Dr.Rathi over phone and briefs him about the matter. He invites her and Avinash to meet him at Nasik, where he is to attend a conference.

Dr.Rathi walks out of the conference hall and cites Kasturi. She approaches him, wishing him before he asks about Avinash. In another half an hour they brief all about their problem and also the proposed solution by Manav. As expected Dr.Rathi wants to know about the credibility of Manav and knowing his background he utters "see, these politically connected people are not safe to deal with. If he cheats, you won't be able to do much about it and your money is gone."

In the current scenario, it is difficult to arrange even a lac. Where will this 12 lac come from? This thought haunts Kasturi throughout the discussion. She badly needs this type of help. Back in her mind, she expects that some other more feasible option should be figured out.

Leaning back on the couch, Dr.Rathi dials a number. By the time it is ringing, he mentions looking at both of them. "Advocate Kailash, he is a good friend of mine, and legal or illegal, he will know all the ways out." Dr.Rathi speaks with Advocate Kailash while Kasturi and Avinash don't mind staring at him and trying to understand the conversation. Disconnecting the call Dr.Rathi says, "What this person Manav is saying is possible but what is the assurance that he is really capable of doing this?" Kasturi tries to suggest that if Kailash can help them out with this?. Dr.Rathi mentions that he is a big shot and if at all he can help then the amount would be much higher than quoted by Manav. Another question is that how is Manav going to manage with this so-called small amount then?

Power of Subconscious Mind

Vikram, the owner of this bungalow is presented handcuffed in the court after about 5-6 hearings. Avinash and Kasturi are also called in front of the Judge and Adv. Sharma passes some agreement to the court registrar, he in turn passes the document to the judge who glances at it and returns. Document travels through the same route to Vikram who signs it and then it is also signed by Avinash and Kasturi.

It is a court order, a Memorandum of Understanding (MOU) which allows Vikram to give single key possession of the said bungalow to them.

Vikram, an Engineering graduate has been behind bars for quite some time now and they didn't mention this to Avinash during the finalisation or during accepting the advance. It was only his mother, sister, and her husband who were always physically present. After paying a handsome amount of advance Avinash had discovered that the papers were with the Bank and that the balance amount needs to be paid to the bank. By this time they had already paid a handsome amount and it was not worth calling off the deal and since bankers looked cooperative and mentioned that they will give single key possession via court hence they had no reason to sense that it would lead to any more problems.

Little did they know that what they have seen till now

was just a trailer and a real movie was yet to be featured!

They are happy to get the possession and take a week for shifting in batches.On the last day they shift all the heavy stuff. Same day Avinash leaves for a business tour and Kasturi is busy settling down the kids and arranging the rooms.

The doorbell rings and she is expecting Neetu, her kid sister. But to her surprise, there is a society watchman at the door. "Madam, the secretary has called you to the society office." She asks about the reason for the same but couldn't get any satisfactory answer. By this time she is aware that the seller is not a genuine guy and hence she calls the cable operator who helped in finalising this deal to join her to the society office as he is also a known person there and he may be of some use to share some information if required. It doesn't take much time for Kasturi to figure out that he is ignoring her as he is not willing to join..

It is past 8pm and security person again ring the doorbell saying that the secretary is waiting for her in the office. She walks with him to the office on the mezzanine floor above the club house of this society comprising 72 bungalows.

She enters the room and greets the person sitting on the other side of the table. "Yes madam, have a seat" he utters. She pulls the chair while 3-4 persons stand behind her. She feels little more than awkward but doesn't show that on her face. Without wasting time in any introduction this middle-aged person addresses her "You have not informed us and moved in without society's permission." Before he could continue further Kasturi presents him with acknowledgement of the letter they submitted to society that they are shifting. He is not aware of this letter and it is visible on his face. Not getting much scope to argue he just says, "You need to vacate this place within 2 days else I will see to it that guards don't allow you to enter the premises." Kasturi is shocked hearing this and gets up in fury "We have bought this place and have a court order for the same. Why two days sir? If possible stop me if you can right now." She leaves the room without even watching out for his reaction. It is not understandable how someone can talk this way in this type of society? Kasturi senses that there are many angles of complications concerning this place. She is anxious to know but is still relaxed and relying on the MOU.

As she narrates this to Avinash, he too shares his homework on this bungalow with her.The owner of this bungalow is behind bars for 90Crore fraud involving many such properties in that area. The property is under litigation and many members of the society were offering the concerned bank a much lesser price than what was to be recovered from this property. They could only relate this angle to Kasturi's experience with the society's secretary.

But, this was not all. While there were many legal formalities to be carried out that kept them occupied there is also some downfall in the business with demonetization declared.

In the middle of the night at around 1pm the doorbell rings. Kasturi is not bothered as she is fast asleep. It is only the next morning Avinash hands over a piece of paper with a contact number mentioned on it saying "Last night security person came and mentioned that some policemen visited us at night and as we were not here he gave his contact number and asked to call back. Kasturi is surprised "Police, why?" "No idea, just call and check if anything serious let me know" he says so and leaves for Nasik.

While in the office, post-lunch Kasturi recollects that she has to call that number. She dials and in no time the call is received. "Sir, I am Kasturi." Before she could say anything further, there is a heavy voice from the other side "Madam, you cannot enter this bungalow without permission, you have not submitted a letter at the police station." Kasturi sounds annoyed "What are you talking about? What letter?" He continues "We have received a complaint that you have illegally occupied bungalow no.3 without any intimation to Society office and Police as well." Kasturi almost raises her voice "illegally?" she sighs before continuing "we have a court order and we have purchased this bungalow and are not tenants hence there is no such requirement as I understand." The so-called policeman is adamant and says "ok, come and meet me at the police check post." Kasturi asks "which Police station?" "No, don't come to the police station, come at the police check post" he responds. "I will not come to any police check post and if you want to see documents I shall come to the Police station" Kasturi blasts him and he hangs up before she could complete her sentence.

Post that conversation this number is switched off or not reachable for many days. They could relate this episode to either foul play by some other prospective buyer from society or the owner himself. It is difficult to believe that something like this was happening. But right now they have enough to deal with and this matter goes unattended further from their side.

It is been almost a month and more since the MOU is signed in the court but there is no further movement from Vikram's family or Advocate. Sharma while Avinash is busy following up with the bankers, Kuturi is persistent in following up with Vikram's lawyer for the rest of the formalities to be completed.

One fine day, Avinash receives a call from Advocate Sharma that both of them need to reach the local municipal Hospital at around 11.30 am. Vikram is not keeping well and hence he is to visit the hospital for his treatment. There they can meet him and take the signature on the Application to be submitted to the Registrar's Office for registration of the sales deed. They reach well in time but need to wait for almost an hour by the time the police van comes and halts and Vikram comes out of it. He is handcuffed and police unlock the cuffs and set his hands free. His family waits there in one corner to meet him. Vikram's mother hands over the tiffin to him. He takes it and sits in one corner and eats while other members talk to him.

That scene is so touchy, Kasturi expresses to Avinash

"Why would he have put himself in this situation? Look at his mother, at this age what she has to go through." "Greed leads men to this road. Anyways, I hope we get out of this type of meetings with him soon" Avinash expresses.

Vikram's family leaves and he walks toward Avinash. This is their first meeting. Vikram is so normal while talking to them. It doesn't look like he has come in a police van and all that. Kasturi shows her concern "heard that you are unwell. Hope nothing serious." Vikram laughs "nothing actually, I just need to manage a little bit so that I am allowed out of jail, then this is the best place. I get an hour or so to spend with my family, talk to them." Kasturi is surprised to see that Vikram's face has no regrets whatsoever. Avinash looks at Kasturi and in an attempt to avoid her further queries he utters "Where are the papers?" Kasturi takes papers out of her bag, Vikram takes a book out of his small bag saying "Avinash, I have something to give you and like signing an autograph he writes on it 'with Love from' and signs. Holding the book in one hand and pen in another Vikram mentions, "I learned that you both are Engineers too. To both of them surprise, Vikram too had the same degree from the same College. He was just 3 years senior to them. He continues "I used to donate Rs.20-25 lacs to some trust and I have taken my parents to the topmost point on earth by a private helicopter. You know how much it costs? Now I have to gather 25-30 thousand from some or the other friend to manage a so-called medical check-up. See how time changes." He hands over the book to Avinash. Avinash takes papers from Kasturi and hands it over to Vikram and he signs them and returns. Vikram glances at the book which is in Kasturi's hands and says looking at Avinash "You should read it." Both are least interested in the book though they say that they will surely do. Without even looking at the cover Kasturi just put it in her bag before leaving.

Way back home is full of Vikram's discussion and his 90Cr fraud and his Economic offences department cases and all that. What they just hope is that this all ends as early as possible because all these follow-up is killing their time.

Finally, the day of registration arrives. Kasturi doesn't forget to visit the temple while on the way to the registration office. Both of them are so happy that finally registration is taking place and they will be done with this Vikram fellow. They reach the Registration office half an hour before the scheduled time. They are aware that Vikram is to be brought there in a Police Van. It is 11am and they are expecting Vikram anytime now.Mhatre, representative from the bank's recovery department is already waiting even before they reach. Avinash looks at him with a smile on his face saying "oh, we thought we are reaching early but you are here before us? Both laugh. He says "More than you we are keen on this registration. With this, we will be recovering at least some amount from this crook."

It is still taking time and three of them go to the

canteen for tea. Mhatre, tell them which all properties belong to Vikram all over the area and how he has done all these frauds. This is shocking for Avinash and Kasturi. By now with all these follow-ups with the bankers they have developed a good repo with them.

Three of them wait and wait till it is lunchtime but there is no sign of Vikram. They try to call Adv. Sharma, and he conveys that it all depends on the availability of the Police and Police van and that there can be a delay but he will be there for registration for sure. They have no option but to wait. Talking to Adv. Sharma doesn't stop Kasturi from getting anxious. Finally, around 4pm they see the police van crossing the road from the other side and entering the Registration office premises. They are bored by now and all that enthusiasm for the most awaited event is lost in the past 5hours. Unlike last time they saw Vikram getting down handcuffed and all. This time it is not so. Vikram comes out of the van in a neat, briskly ironed full white cotton Shirt and trousers. Kasturi utters "He is a prisoner or a politician? Avinash holds her hand saying "Come, don't analyse." They walk inside the building and straight to the counter. Carrying out all formalities brings back the excitement in Kasturi. They happily return home thinking that one chapter is over and now just the bank loan procedure may take another month or so. They had already enquired with their bankers and got the list of documents to be submitted. Most of the documents Avinash had kept ready.

Another Chapter of this lesson begins with the actual submission of papers to the bank. There is more in store for them yet.

Their bankers reject the loan proposal because they find another sale deed in the search history. Bankers need this cancellation deed now. The Mortgage bank is also surprised to know this but for the matter of fact this is a sure shot negligence from them. How much ever bankers feel bad about the matter the fact is that they were in soup due to banker's negligence. There are suggestions from family, friends and lawyers to file a case against the bank too but it would only lead to more legal fights.

Kasturi's follow-ups with 'The Mr.Manav' start taking toll on her patience now. It has been 3-4 times she visited Kolhapur. He makes her stay there for 2-3 days on most of her visits saying we are to meet some authority, submit some documents, sometimes need her passport size photographs, sometimes need her signature on some documents. All these are just requirements from him and she has no option but to listen to him and visit Kolhapur, wait for 2-3 days and take all those excuses about him being busy, and return without meeting him or carrying out any formality for the work. By now Kasturi is fed up and wants to give up but she holds on a bit every time with a bit of hope. At times chats begin with her work-related matters and end up with Manav dragging it to personal interest.

Sometimes being too optimistic is also not good. It is

very important to know where to cut the string. But then, was it so easy? Looking at the tree from far off and not feeling bad about the shedding leaves is different but shedding off hopes is not so. The situation sometimes arises that even an unfaithful hope is capable of holding you together when 'not giving up' is the only right thing for that moment.

Avinash recollects their previous neighbours while they stayed in a rented house just after marriage, who happened to be a well-known lawyer. But these many days they were not in touch. No address, no contact number. But, Avinash roughly recollects them mentioning their address during their last meeting.

He has no idea if he was recollecting it correctly and if they were still there. Both of them decide to look for them.

They leave the office an hour early and to their good luck, they land up at the correct address.

Coming out of the elevator on the 17th floor they ring the bell and the door opens to a completely messy living room. They look at each other smiling with an expression 'still the same.' The housemaid serves them water while the tall, beautiful lady comes out in excitement. She hugs Kasturi saying "After so long, you never called me. But, how can you call? I didn't give you my number. How did you know this address then?" Her questions are endless.

Those days they were next-door neighbours and after listening to Kasturi's matter she immediately calls her husband "Kasturi and Avinash are here. How much ever busy you are, meet them immediately as they are in trouble. I am sending them to your office. Do whatever you can to solve their problem." They feel a bit relieved and leave with a warm goodbye.

Wadekar's office is just 5mins walk from his residence. They climb stairs leading to the second floor of an old building. At least 18-20 pairs of footwear outside the office made it look shabby. They enter and the young boy looks at them asking "Mr.Avinash?" Avinash nods "yes." Kasturi looks around noticing that there is no place to sit at all. The young boy takes them directly to Adv.Wadekar's cabin. He looks at them from the upper edge of his spectacles. Not even a pinch of any expressions on his face as usual. "Come sit, what's the problem? My wife called saying "you both are in some problem."

Knowing Advocate's nature Avinash doesn't waste time on any formalities and comes directly to the point. Explaining Adv.Wadekar with absolutely no response from him throughout gives Kasturi a feeling that maybe he didn't like them visiting this way. She is aware that even back then they hardly had any interaction with him. For that matter, they must have met him only once or twice throughout their stay over a year.

Advocate Wadekar is finally vocal about the matter. He closes the flap of his laptop and picks up the pen from the pen holder with his left hand. Start scribbling on the writing pad saying "so, no.1 you have already paid Rs.60 lacs." He writes Rs.60 lacs and circles it continuing "no.2 owner has already sold this property to someone else too and you need his cancel deed and no.3 he is absconding." Avinash replies "Yes." Adv.Wadekar calls that young boy but his voice hardly goes out of this room "bring their footwears I shall keep and worship them, they have done such a blunder" His words hurt. Avinash still manages to smile taking it lightly but Kasturi reacts "We approached you with the hope that since you are a lawyer you may know a way out." Advocate bounces back "there is no way out. Not only the owner but even the mortgage bankers have cheated you. You should give up on this matter, leave whatever amount is gone and start again peacefully. Else, such cases go on and on for generations with no outcome." He senses that he has been a bit harsh on them and talks to Avinash enquiring about their whereabouts for all these years and Kasturi is lost in her 'how to go about it further' mode.

Kasturi has to travel to Kolhapur and it is hardly 15mins meeting. She is aware that most of her time is going to be spent waiting. It is been quite some time since she wanted to go through the book given by Vikram during their first meeting. She opens her drawer and takes and puts this book in her bag. As expected her meeting winds up in less than 15 mins and it is almost 4hrs for her train. Relaxing in the waiting room she takes out this book. Complete yellow colour with the bold red font 'THE POWER OF SUBCONSCIOUS MIND'. She has never heard any such thing before but the title definitely made sense and seems relatable as well.

It happens to one and all, lots of time we go through some process, some system but we are not aware of what that is. She can relate the context to her own. The way she used to look at the bungalow and thought that someday they would buy a bigger house which would be worth waiting for all these years probably attracted her to this place. She thinks if it is so, be it. If subconsciously I attracted this house then the same formula will take us out of these legal issues, we just need to believe and act. This understanding refrains from giving up even when it seems to be impossible. 'THE POWER OF SUBCONSCIOUS MIND', concept or reality? She is not to judge but starts believing as she reads and receives it through the days, months and years.

It is Despande; CEO of the bank eventually takes responsibility for the negligence of his staff and calls both of them once in his office. Accompanied by Mhatre they reach Deshpande's office who welcomes both of them warm-heartedly. They discuss the matter and conclude that there is no way but to find out this third person and get the agreement cancelled.

Kasturi has a tough time not looking at his shining bald as they greet goodbye to Mhatre.

This is a challenge for the bankers. Kasturi and Avinash are relieved for a very short time because the ball is in the banker's court now.

Bankers are to get the cancel deed done, and then it is

going to be just the matter of requesting their bankers to reconsider their case and as promised by their relationship manager they would consider that once the cancel deed is done.

They are trying to focus on their business back as it suffered due to all these issues. No more than 15days pass and Mhatre calls up early in the morning. Kasturi looks at Avinash saying "It is Mhatre." She wishes him good morning and he too greets her back. There is a short conversation that ends up with Kasturi saying "oh, is it? How can we organise that now?" Looking at Avinash she mentions "that third person has been arrested" Avinash exclaims, arrested!

Kasturi explains "Mhatre says that this person too is a big fraud and was underground for more than 6months. Sangli police caught him at some remote village." Avinash is not bothered to hear about his whereabouts, he is only interested in his work. "What did Mhatre say? Avinash questions and is also shocked to hear Kasturi saying "He is demanding Rs.7 lacs for cancelling his agreement." Kasturi is not convinced about this and she expresses that it is the banker's fault, why should we pay for their negligence." Avinash analyses the situation in his way and convinces Kasturi by saying," we don't have a choice unless until this agreement is cancelled we won't get a loan at all. Bankers can fool us but these people don't look like they cheated.

They both talk for a long time trying to figure out how and where to organise this amount from.

Eventually, zeros down to some option and Kasturi calls Mhatre. Avinash looks at her while she talks "we could organise only Rs.3.5 lacs. This house's legal complications have put us in a difficult situation." Avinash smiles at her hearing this.

The next day around the same time Mhatre calls and tells that the person is not ready to negotiate but he could convince the bank to bear 50% and that the bank agreed.

They reach the registration office well in time but notice Mhatre and the third person already at the entrance. Kasturi raises her query to Avinash "they said he was caught in Sangli but he is not accompanied by Police, how come? "Avinash feels she is bothering unnecessarily and warns her "now please don't start questioning them, give that cash." Kasturi takes out a packet from her handbag and hands it over to him." Avinash walks toward Mhatre while Kasturi keeps observing from a distance.

Driving back home Kasturi mentions to Avinash that she feels looking at the scenario at the registration office that Mhatre gave only our Rs.3.5 lacs and that probably they lied, it was either only this amount to be given or they negotiated and lied to us that it is Rs.7 lacs and they are paying 50%. Avinash too agrees to this as he also senses so. There is no option so they decide to let go without taking it up to the bankers.

Finally even with the cancelled deed in hand, not only their bankers but many other banks refuse to sanction a home loan as it is already one year passed since the agreement; they are no longer eligible for a home loan. Moreover, their finances dropped as business suffered due to change in the market scenario as well.

After the rejection of loan proposals from their official bankers, they approach most of the banks and everyone goes through the process of documentation, login, valuation, and eventually denies going ahead. By now Avinash is fed up with preparing copies of documents, approaching banks. Three months down the line and practically all the banks have by now rejected loans to them.

Deshpande is the only person talking today with all possible options while Kasturi, Avinash and Mhatre sit calm in front of him with no options to suggest. By now Deshpande also sounds frustrated as he was the one who forced them to occupy the bungalow. At the same time despite every attempt, their recovery is still not done. Kasturi suggests, "Sir, property papers are with you and you are also keen on settling this account, so why don't you consider giving us a home loan. For you, this chapter is closed and we too are relieved then." Deshpande looks at Mhatre "Let's try this out." Mhatre nods in acceptance. Deshpande instructs Mhatre to take all financials from Avinash, check on them, and that they meet again in two days.

They meet again, just to conclude that it was not possible as cooperative banks can only fund Rs.70 lacs and the said amount was much more. Mhatre looks at Avinash enquiring "Can you arrange the balance amount?" Avinash is instant in his reply "No way sir, the difference is huge; we can't arrange this big amount." Kasturi argues that just shift his loan to our account and we shall pay, but in vain.Hence it is concluded that this option is also not workable.

What next? As for bankers, though they have a good repo with them, the banker's priority is recovery. Kasturi and Avinash will not leave the house now as they have a court order for possession and have paid a hefty amount already.

Vishwanathan, a private agent calls on Kasturi's phone offering to work on their case and assuring him to get it done. Avinash is in no mood to make another set of documents ready. By this time both of them are so frustrated that they feel it won't be done at all so why waste time and money over another attempt. Unwillingly, they submit documents to Vishwanathan and another sequence of login, valuation, personal discussion, etc, etc takes place. Vishwanathan along with this non-banking finance company's representative visits them and he too mentions that a Housing loan is not possible now. A sequence of problems does not wish to end at all. All that charm and happiness of shifting in this house seems to be under many more layers yet.

Deshpande calls up Avinash and checks if he can visit his office. He doesn't sound polite and friendly as always. By now they are aware that these bankers are also in trouble and may take some stand now. Avinash visits Deshpande and returns home frustrated. Kasturi teases Avinash saying "so how's your best friend? How much love did he show today?" Avinash looks angrily at her uttering "They say they have tried their level best and now if we don't arrange payment we will need to vacate the bungalow." Kasturi gets furious to hear this and keeps on blabbering throughout preparing dinner that bankers are responsible and they cannot take this stand now.

Finally, Vishwanathan comes up with the option of getting a 'Loan gainst Property (LAP)' from this finance company and after a couple of joint discussions, they conclude to explore this option. It is taking too long for all these possibilities to be figured out and work on them though. They are well aware that since the matter is out of even Deshpande's control, he may not cooperate now.

They decide to take legal advice yet again and Avinash travels to Akola to visit a lawyer friend who in turn directs Avinash to another friend of his who looks into property matters. This lawyer is very helpful and prepares a notice which can be issued to the Bankers if they take any stand to vacate the bungalow. His advice is that, before they take any legal action against you for not being able to settle their dues yet, you should do so because you are in trouble due to their negligence. Though friendly and helpful this too costs them quite a bit of money and all this adds on to the extra cost they have to shed for this place. Both of them are not keen on taking this step. They keep the notice as the last option praying that something should get worked out before this step is required to be taken.

One morning Mhatre calls Avinash to convey Deshpande's invite for Avinash for tea in his office. Kasturi is not very keen to join but Avinash insists saying "Today Deshpande may not be soft as always with us, I could figure out from Mhatre's tone and surprisingly he will not be there today. I think he is purposefully trying to avoid being present."

They arrive at Deshpande's office. Kasturi notices light reflecting on his bald head as usual and smiles to herself. Lots of times she would wonder and think "how can i notice these silly things even in such a tense situation?" She is surprised at her own behaviour. But, that's how she is!

As they occupy their seats and green tea is served to them as usual both notice that Deshpande is not in his regular tone as expected. He begins looking at Kasturi and pointing at Avinash "You know I love this man. In the whole of my life I have never met any such person who always has a smile on his face. But, that is not going to help with my recovery." "Sir you know very well how hard we are trying to get loan sanctioned and even your bank, using your contacts with other banks too couldn't do it" Kasturi defends immediately.

Deshpande turns to Avinash and almost warns them "You will need to give me a deadline when you will pay. I cannot wait indefinitely. I am also answerable to management." Avinash just wants to wind up as there's going to be no outcome of this talk. He politely mentions "ok sir, give us a couple of days and we will get back." But Deshpande is in no mood to conclude the meeting without a fixed date and he continues "no, you have to commit to some date before you leave today else I won't mind having dinner here with you both" he sarcastically laughs and pauses seeing their slightly angry faces. Kasturi is all set to argue but Avinash taps her foot while asking her to calm down. Avinash gets up saying "I will just call Vishwanathan and check what the current status is, just give me a couple of minutes I will be back." Kasturi too gets up, looks at Deshpande and keeps her bag down before walking behind Avinash suggesting that they are not running away. Out of his office, they look at each other and Kasturi says "good that we too are prepared with the draft notice. She calls Vishwanathan to check the status." Vishwanthan doesn't have any concrete answer yet and this makes both of them sad. Before Avinash could finish his call with Vishwanathan, Kasturi already connects with their lawyer to mention bank's stand. Avinash looks at her to check whom she was talking to and she tells him "He says we should go ahead with issuing notice to them." They mutually decide that they will tell that they will try to settle within 8-10 days else they are free to do what they feel appropriate.

They enter Deshpande's cabin. Avinash is ready to make the statement as decided but Kasturi is fast to say while Avinash looks at her with surprise as she speaks "sir, one month. Give us one more month and if we are not in a position to organise a loan you guide us on how we should go about it further. Not giving him any room to discuss further Avinash with his smile sums up "sir, you have been generously helping and guiding us and you know we are trying. Please agree and we will keep you posted about the developments." Deshpande unwillingly says "ok" but it is just for both of you, had it been someone else I wouldn't have agreed." They knew that despite their negligence Deshpande was pretending as if he was doing some favour but they don't mind it in the interest of avoiding arguments. As it is this matter is consuming a lot of their time and energy putting their business on the back seat at times.

15days passed this meeting and it looks like things were falling in place. Vishwanathan confirms that their case has finally got legal clearance and it is just a matter of disbursement in another 4-5days time. Finally, they feel relieved.

But was it a relief or just another thread added in the entangled bunch? It is yet to be known.

Another technical issue arises.

Since it is a LAP, the finance company demands property papers before disbursement and this is again not possible as bankers won't release them before their amount is received in their account. After a series of talks with both the finance company and the bankers, Kasturi manages to convince both of them and they agreed to exchange papers and demand a draft of the said amount across the table.

It is Friday and early morning they get ready. Avinash

calls Mhatre which is just a reminder call for today's final meeting. There is no need for any reminder as Mhatre is also desperately waiting for this time. For Kasturii and Avinash, their property was free from litigation which many predicted would never happen or will take a lifetime of court visits and for Mhatre it was the closure of one more recovery case.

At the bank at 11.30am all of them sitting across the table with their hearts filled with different tastes of satisfaction and all faces lit with pleasant smiles. Ramesh from the Finance company takes out the demand draft and places it on the table. Mhatre hands over the property papers to Ramesh who has already gone through them physically a week before this day, again turning these same pages looking briefly at them, and says "Yes, Fine. Here's your Demand Draft." Mhatre gets up and with a slight sentimental tone requests Ramesh and Vishwanathan "We all are thankful that you have tried hard and got this loan sanctioned but I would like to receive this from Kasturi and Avinash. "This case was difficult but we were able to conclude due to their strong approach." He continues "I have been working in the recovery department for 18 years now but I have never met people like them, they look tiny but are so strong and determined. Despite our mistakes, they were always polite and helpful to us." Avinash and Kasturi look at each other thinking of the notice they had already kept ready which remains unutilized, the amount they paid to the lawyer was just down the drain but they are really happy that the notice remains un-served and unknown to Mhatre.

Avinash gets up and without Ramesh's permission picks the demand draft from the table, looks at Kasturi, she too stands up and they hand it over to Mhatre with wet eyes. Mhatre's sentiments are also clearly visible to everyone in that room. Vishwanathan gets up and pats Avinash's back with a smile of appreciation before leaving with Ramesh. Kasturi and Avinash too pick up their bags but Mhatre stops them saying "Let's have coffee" and rings a bell for the office boy. Sipping the warm coffee with the experiences they have gone through past one and a half years is an experience the three of them will never forget in their lifetime.

Mhatre comes out of his cabin along with them. He holds Avinash's hand and asks him to wait. Looks at Kasturi saying "Madam" Kasturi looks back. Mhatre addresses all his staff clapping his hands so that all of them sitting in their cubicles notice him "Everyone please come here." He repeats it till every person is there in front of him. He continues "I want to introduce you to this couple. Many of you must have seen them coming to our office regularly throughout the past year." Mhatre elaborates how he is thankful to them for patiently handling this and even expresses his gratitude as he feels it is because of them their recovery is possible." He starts clapping and everyone follows him. Kasturi and Avinash feel a bit embarrassed. They pass a smile to a few known and few unknown faces standing there.

With whatever intentions Vikram gifted the book to them, Kasturi discovered the Power of the subconscious mind. Believed in it and they sailed through the patch when even experts advised them to quit. Least did she know that, the concept is going to help her sail through further challenges as well.

On the way back home, Avinash informs his family and friends about the big news while Kasturi just recollects.

Her father is holding small Kasturi and opens his fist to free a tiny dragonfly saying "You should never give up and always stand strong then problems fly just like this." She smiles to herself with wet eyes as her younger version runs behind the dragonfly.

The Confidence-Man

Kasturi is sitting at the Saibaba Temple since morning aarti, with Rs.7lacs cash in her bag. She did not move a bit until it was time for afternoon aarti. All the while, her mind and heart prayed with great faith, "If this work is not to be done, please don't let this money go to him."

Manav was known to her for just eight months via a deal for equipment purchased by some trust in Kolhapur. Kasturi was not so friendly with him initially, though. He always dropped some or another message, sometimes just wishing her.

It was a regular interaction for two months or more during the deal and she didn't mind his in between irrelevant chats. She didn't realise it when she became friendly with him over chat. He never crossed the decency limit, and when she learned he was almost a decade younger to her, the conversation became even more relaxed. All the while, their communication was limited to phone calls, emails, and WhatsApp.

Today, with the entire financial burden and still managing to get a personal loan of seven lacs was not easy, but the bankers managed to sanction this. All these four hours in front of Sai Baba Idol, Kasturi recollected her first visit to Manav's office.

Her local engineer Rakesh is accompanying her but, while she is sitting across the table opposite Manav, the presence of his office boy and Rakesh didn't bother him and he keep on staring at Kasturi for a couple of moments, making it embarrassing for all in the cabin. Kasturi with raised voice waves, taps on the table with a pen and directs a bunch of papers towards him "Hello, these are all reports. Let me know if you can help us with settling the balance payment."

She also recollects how Manav in the name of helping her out with her property matter, called her to Pune.

Kasturi takes a day off as a banker who is supposed to visit for a valuation of her house. Post lunch she gets a call asking for guidance to reach her place, she guides the bank person and he is there within 5 mins. While showing him the rooms and balcony her phone rings which she is holding in her left hand, she quickly receives it without checking who it was to avoid disturbance to Varun's sleep. She receives a call from Manav. The inspection guy asks her if the balcony and terrace area is included in the Carpet area calculation. She says "only 50% of the area is included in carpet area calculation." She notices someone is on line and checks "Yes, Hello, who is this?" other side questions "oh, so deleted my number?" Kasturi justifies "No, I picked up in a hurry and didn't notice your name on screen "Hi, how are you?"

Manav checks with her about what was she talking about carpet area and all and she just briefs him about her situation related to the bungalow and Manav is ready with the solution, "Do one thing, you carry on with your bank but also give me one set of documents and I shall try, maybe you get a better rate because of my contacts. I am coming to Pune on Wednesday. Do come with your documents, let's see."

Kasturi talks to Manav over the intercom from the reception of his hotel. She refuses to visit his room, but he insists that they sit in his room and discuss it. She reaches his room and has to wait out while housekeeping takes another couple of minutes to organise the room. She enters as they leave and occupies the chair next to the study table. Greeting each other sounds formal, unlike their telephonic talks. Manav senses discomfort in her body language and tries to ease her discomfort by explaining himself "I am trying to avoid some people and hence didn't want to sit in the lobby or restaurant. Don't be uncomfortable. Katuri just nods. Her phone rings, and its Avinash checking if she reached safely. Kasturi takes out all her property documents and account statements and hands them over to Manav. He takes it from her and places it on the table. He makes a call to someone saying "Yes, I have received documents. Will you please send someone to collect them?"

Before Kasturi would try to say anything, Manav gets up from his chair saying "I will just be back" and handing over the restaurant menu card he continues, "please order something for you till I come back?." "Ok, by that time, let me wait in the lobby then" Kasturi makes an unsuccessful attempt to get out of the room. Manav insists that she should wait in the room and then leaves.

Waiting for him in that room for half an hour seems like a long time. She calls him a couple of times and he doesn't receive the call. She gets up in anxiety as the door chuckles and opens. Manav enters the room and looks at her saying, "Sit, ordered anything?" "Manav I need to push off. It is been almost two hours" Kasturi requests. "Let the person come and pick up your papers, and then you can leave'" he again suggests. He leaves the room again and this time it has been more than an hour. Now Kasturi is upset. She gets up and first just wants to get out of this room. She comes out and feels relaxed. Walking through the corridor, taking the elevator and then the main lobby, Kasturi is about to leave the hotel, and Manav appears in front of her from nowhere.

He is just coming to pick up your papers in 10 minutes, if you are not comfortable in the room, we will wait in the lobby. Kasturi murmurs "that's what I said in the morning." Manav looks at her with expressions depicting that he heard what she said. She is not bothered.

Sitting on the coach, she is not able to figure out what Manav is up to. It is been 4pm and she has been here with the documents since 10 am. No one came to take her papers till now, and the whole day Manav is making her sit and wait while disappearing intermittently.

Finally he comes and sits on the adjacent coach. Again trying to prove himself he says, "Don't worry, I will get your property matter sorted out." By now, Kasturi is in no mood to even discuss this. All she is thinking about is getting back home now. Manav surprises her with his next statement, "You are a very good female and very beautiful. I mean, you have a very beautiful smile, a very sweet voice, but you are not my type." A mob approaches them before she could even raise her eyebrows. An elderly person in a white shirt and an off-white Nehru jacket with many people following him comes toward Manav and hugs him as Manav stands up. "It is nice to see you. Some important work must have brought you here. Big shots like you are hardly seen at our place." Manav is not willing to have any discussions with this person and just says, "Yes, I have some important work." That person greets and leaves.

Kasturi raises her finger trying to say something, but Manav doesn't allow her to speak. Resting back on the couch, he says "You know who he was? He is the mayor of this city. That's why I didn't want to sit in the lobby. Someone or other will continue to annoy." Kasturi picks up her bag and is ready to leave. Manav sounds upset. "You can't leave like that." Kasturi questions, "What do you mean, you can't leave like that? Manav makes an unsuccessful attempt to make her wait. "No, we need to discuss your property matter." Kasturi just sits on the edge of the couch saying, "Listen, I have been here since the morning and I am just waiting for this so-called person to come and pick up my documents from you and all that you were trying to say was not very appropriate. Do not try to cross your limit. I am here sitting with you as you have always been decent."

Manav gets desperate. "We need to talk." Kasturi senses something is wrong with him. He doesn't look normal. She tries to tell him that they can talk later on the phone and just turns around and leaves.Her diver is waiting outside and gets the car as soon as he notices her coming out. She apologises to the driver, "Sorry, it got late. I didn't expect this. You can take a leave tomorrow." The driver is polite in his reply, "No problem, Madam."

Kasturi calls Avinash and informs him about her day's experience, omitting Manav's irrelevant statements though. Just five minutes pass as they leave and Kasturi's phone rings. It is Manav. She just looks at her phone and places it back on the dashboard. It gets disconnected and rings and disconnects and rings till she takes it and answers, "Sorry, my phone was in my bag." Manav sounds indifferent. "How can you leave like this? You can't leave me alone and go just like that. I have been *waiting to meet you for months and you just left me alone. "Kasturi is shocked to hear all this. All this while, when they talked over the phone and chatted, he never said any such thing and was always decent to trust and talk with. Kasturi is feeling sad about all this because, by this time she had started taking him as a good friend. She disconnects. He calls again, and she again disconnects. Her driver witnesses her awkward situation and says, "Madam, I will park the car on one side. You talk to this person then we will leave. She nods in acceptance. The driver is about to get out of the car so that she can complete her call, but she asks him to be there and she gets out of the car looking at the continuously ringing phone. She finally picks it up "Don't disconnect Kasturi, you are so good. I like you very much. The first time I saw you in my office, or rather the first time I heard your voice, I fell in love with you."*

Kastur yells, "What nonsense, Manav, I thought you were trying to help me." Manav defends himself "of course, I am trying to help. I will do all I can do to solve your problem." "That is not required, we can manage our problems. I seriously looked at you as a good friend Manav, and you ruined it all. It was my mistake that I thought we were friends, and it is alright to take help from you" Kasturi blasts.Manav sounds on the verge of crying, "No, listen to me." Kasturi gets too wild "I don't need your help or guidance. Don't ever call me back. I thought you were a decent guy and hence i talked to you. That was my mistake. You probably thought…"

Manav raises his voice, "Don't say anything further. I am not sorry, but I won't bother you again on this. Kasturi displays her anger, "Thank you so much" and disconnects.

Recollecting all these episodes, sitting in the temple

with the cash they had to organise by taking a personal loan, shakes her trust on Manav.

The afternoon Aarti is done. Kasturi's eyes are almost full of tears. She opens her eyes, and with water rolling down her cheeks she prays to receive some signal from her Sai if this is going to work out or not. She turns to come out of the prayer hall, her phone vibrates and it is Manav. She takes it as a positive signal and feels happy about it. She hurriedly comes out of the hall and receives the call. Manav speaks and then hangs up without waiting for her response.

Just before entering the trust office, Kasturi calls Avinash. Her voice sounds low while asking him once again if they should give the money. Avinash persuades her that she should not think about it too much and should go ahead with it because it is a risk of Rs.7lacs for the hope of recovering from sinking business and avoiding the entire trauma they would go through.

In Manav's cabin at his mentioned time Kasturi is sitting calmly for some time while he makes a few calls. After a brief chat, Kasturi takes out cash from her bag and places it on the table saying "we could manage only 7 lacs." Manav just nods and continue talking generally without taking money. Kasturi has continuous thoughts in her mind.

Is he fooling? Is he trying to take advantage of the situation? She is finding it difficult to cope with all that comes to her mind.

One afternoon while in Kolhapur, finishing all her meetings, it suddenly starts raining. Taking shelter at the nearby shop, Rakesh and Kasturi are talking about the unexpected rain. Suddenly, she notices Manav's message, "It started raining heavily, Safe side yourself." She just smiles at his sentence and ignores it.

They were to meet Manav at the trust office because he had advised Kasturi to submit some proposals to the trust, which was for some big project. Kasturi was trying to crack this deal for a long time. After her experience at Pune, she was not in his touch but this project was submitted to the Trust sometimes back and it eventually had landed on Manav's table.

They are expecting his call throughout the day, but this was the only message received from his end. While Kasturi tried calling him a couple of times, he doesn't pick up at all. Rakesh drops her at the entrance of her hotel and leaves. Her time passes talking to her family, and at around 10.30pm, she receives a call from Manav. She sounds tired. Manav asks, "Ya, hello, can we meet? She replies "I was waiting for your call. I called you twice." Manav tries to clarify "Yes, I was too tied up, so can we meet now?"

"Now, at this time?" she questions.

"I don't get time throughout the day, so we can meet and discuss the project" he repeats. Kasturi is blunt in her reply, "I will not be able to come at this odd hour. Tell me what time I can meet you tomorrow morning." Manav tries to convince her to meet at a restaurant or trust office, saying that he can pick her up and drop her back too. She continues to refuse. She senses that he is upset about it, but she is not bothered.

Early in the morning, before she gets up, there is a message from Manav, "I need to take my father for physiotherapy, so I will be able to meet you only later in the evening." She replies to his message "fine, just ping once you are free. My train is at 8pm."

For the whole of the day, Rakesh and Kasturi roam around the city killing time and waiting for Manav's call, but he doesn't call. In the evening, she calls him but in vain. Rakesh drops her at the station. She arranges her bedding and calls Avinash, venting all her anger on Manav for how he wasted her day.

Lying down on the bed, checking messages before switching off her phone, she notices Manav's message "I love you so much that you cannot imagine and you are not even able to trust me." This message bothers Kasturi.

After her experience in Pune, never did Manav behave this way again, and she was under the impression that he understood his mistake. Now again, he was back on the same track. Kasturi doesn't feel like even replying to his message. After a few minutes, he sends another message. I am coming to Mumbai tomorrow morning. Please send your project report to me. I will call you once I land. She is too annoyed and doesn't bother to respond. Just switches off the phone.

In the morning while deboarding the train, she notices another message from him, sent sometime in the middle of the night saying "Good Night."

She is not willing to send any documents to Manav, but after an hour or two, she keeps on thinking and decides to send her person if Manav calls. Surprisingly, he calls around 10.30 am. He directly mentions, "I just landed in Mumbai and have a return flight at 5pm." I will call you in an hour and let you know where to meet with the file.

She starts feeling that he is just messing around, but the magnitude of the project pushed her to believe that this might work. Manav's message last night is unpleasant, so she decides to visit him and confront him directly about his intermittent behavioural attacks of so-called "Love you and Like yous."

She cancels her couple of meetings lined up for the day, gets ready and then has no option but to wait for his call. She knew he might not call in the first half, but after 2pm she became concerned that if she does not hand over the file today, he might call her to Kolhapur again. She calls him 2-3 times in 10-15 min, but his phone either says "not reachable" or "switched off." At the end of the day, she makes up her mind, whatever the situation is, she is not going to follow up with him any further. She looks forward to hearing from him though.

After a couple of days, she feels like checking up, but it is still the same status on the phone. For the next few days, she makes a couple of attempts just to know that his phone was either switched off or not reachable.

Kasturi is busy trying to follow up with several other trusts for her project, but she is not able to get over the thought that what must have happened to Manav?

He calls her to Kolhapur but doesn't meet. He announces his plan of coming to Mumbai, calls when he lands, and then goes missing. Sometimes she wonders if anything wrong or unfortunate must have happened to him, but she ignores her thoughts.

Kasturi requests him to count the amount she placed on the table. Manav counts the bundles. He takes out one big bag and puts, one by one, seven bundles in it. Then he takes out another bag from the drawer of his table, opens it, and takes out another five bundles and puts them in the same bag saying, "This person has asked for 12 lakhs, so we need to give him 12 lakhs." When you said you could manage only seven then I managed the rest. Kasturi shockingly gets up from her seat, saying, "No, I can't take this money from you." He replies, "Don't bother, there is no other option." Kasturi questions him. But, what is it all about? I am not getting it at all. Your odd message, then you don't meet, disappear, and then one fine day, you call with all these so appropriate details. I am not able to understand anything, Manav."

Manav senses a difference in her voice and looks at her saying "don't dig much, just concentrate on your problem and my solution, the rest of it is irrelevant for now." "Maybe, but how and why do you know all these things?" she asks. Manav responds, "I already told you that you and your family's problems are mine."Kasturi reflexes, "But why? Do you go behind everyone, finding out their problems and suggesting solutions?"

Keeping both the bags down, Manav replies to her, "I

have a very small circle of people who I feel close to and I find their problems and try to do what I can do." He continues, "What was so odd about my message?" Kasturi gives him a slightly angry look while he continues, "You all are the same. You take 'I love you' only in one sense while it is not so, and don't give me that angry look. When you love your parents, your siblings, your husband, your kids, that is fine but, when I express the same love for you, then you feel it is odd. I know about you more than you can think and feel about being part of your life. I want to be an important part of you, just like your other relationships, that is it."

Kasturi, holding her head with both her hands, literally shouts at him, "Enough Manav, no one has talked to me like this. One should keep sense while talking." Manav is not willing to give up today. "Don't try to add other adjectives to my feelings. It is pure love and I am not asking you to marry me" and he laughs aloud continuing "don't worry; I am not a college-going boy that I will run behind you. I very well know how much you love your husband and you have grown-up kids, etc., etc. He is not done yet "I fell in love within 5 minutes when I first saw you, rather sensed something when I just heard you say "hello" on the phone for the first time. You are sweet. Everybody likes you, but not all are true to themselves to mention it to you."

Kasturi gets annoyed "Manav, this is all not very pleasant to hear. You know what I am going through, and I don't know how you know all this. But please don't make it difficult for me to talk to you or follow up with you for this work of mine. Moreover as I said, I take you as my friend. You offered to work together on our project. You offered to help. That is fine, but please don't expect anything else. As it is, I am not as comfortable talking to you as before after listening to all these things from you. Manav's face is blank as she talks. Scratching his head, he offers to drop her, but she denies it and leaves after a calm goodbye.

At this point, Kasturi is more worried about only two things. Concerning the money she gave him and the follow-ups she would have to do with him. With whatever he said, the latter one bothers her the most.

In the evening post other meetings; Kasturi has another couple of hours for her train. She asks Rakesh to leave. She just wants to sit in Sai Baba temple all alone with no company, just herself. Her thoughts keep wandering, sometimes giving her hope and sometimes making her feel low. She keeps on looking at Sai Baba's idol from a distance. Not feeling stable emotionally, she gets up and walks down to the railway station. The piercing noise of that busy and crowded street is unable to suppress the one inside her as she walks this long stretch till the station.

The road ahead is not known. It is beyond anyone's capacity to know what will happen tomorrow. One cannot choose 'tomorrow' and cannot change 'yesterday'. Hence, it is very important that 'today' be lived wisely. It is said that destiny cannot be changed.

You have no control over it. But the path can be made comfortable by making the right decisions, probably!

But can we even choose the path?

It had been a year and a half since her existing business too was seeing low sales. Several visits to the customers, finalisation meetings, but eventually orders failed to come. All these years, she has not experienced this. Even while in Kolhapur to follow up with Manav, she and Rakesh would visit their existing customers and even new doctors throughout the day.

It is the third day of her visit to Kolhapur, and Kasturi's train is at 8.30 pm. Kasturi and Rakesh are tired and couldn't have anything for lunch due to back-to-back meetings.

They enter a restaurant and are about to order some snacks. She picks up the menu card and hands it over to Rakesh, asking him to order. Just while the waiter comes and stands to take the order, Kasturi receives a call from Manav saying "Sorry, I had to travel out of Kolhapur. I am just reaching; meet me at the trust office at 8 pm." My train leaves at 8.00 pm. It will be too late for me Manav" she responds. He gives another option, "Ok, come home in half an hour" and hangs up. Immediately calls back, "Listen, you will be safe don't worry. My mother is also here" and laughs sarcastically. Kasturi disconnects. She talks with Rakesh about it, and eventually both of them leave without eating anything.

Rakesh gets down from his bike in front of a seven-story building. Rakesh gets a call from a technician because he is facing some issue with the machine operations and needs to guide the technician on the phone. Rakesh suggests that he shall wait downstairs and complete his call. Kasturi does not want to go to Manav's place alone. But, it is also important for Rakesh to attend to his call. Though Rakesh and Kasturi never discussed it, he is aware of the discomfort and insecurity she is facing. He suggests, "Madam, you go and I will call you in another 10 minutes." "Tell me if everything is fine, or else I will immediately come up." Kasturi nods and leaves.

Kasturi gets out of a small elevator on the 4th floor. Coming out, she turns left and looks for room 401 as mentioned by Manav. She looks for the doorbell but couldn't find one. She knocks on the door and hears Manav's voice, "Here, this way." She looks for Manav and he is on the right side of the elevator. There is another room also marked as 401. Manav notices confusion on her face and explains "that door opens to my terrace. This is the main door."Kasturi responds while entering his house, following him "oh, oK." She intentionally leaves the door wide open. The beautiful and well-maintained terrace garden catches her attention as she walks into the living room, which is not very big but beautifully decorated with paintings, wooden pieces, and lots of feng shui items as well. She doesn't get any negative vibes about his intentions and feels at ease. Manav notices that her eyes are searching for his mother. He smiles and mentions, "Mom, just returned from her cousin's place. She is having a bath." Kasturi passes a tiny smile as Manav gets her a glass of water. Kasturi looks at her wristwatch, saying "it is already 7pm, my train…." Before she could complete her sentence, Manav speaks "Yes, I know your train is at 8.30." Kasturi's phone rings and she understands that it is Rakesh's call. She quickly picks up and replies, "Yes, will come in 15-20 mins." Manav continues, "You will need a local office here because they will only help local businesses". Kasturi mentions, "Yes, Rakesh is here and we have been working here for 15 years now." Manav further explains, "You need a registered or operating office here." He concludes "look for a small place on rent, make an agreement and give it to me. We need to submit an agreement." Before Kasturi could further say anything, there is a noise of a door lock opening. Kasturi looks in that direction. A lady in her late 60s, with a soothing personality and a pleasant smile, walks toward her. Kasturi gets up from her place and smiles at her, wishing her a good evening. The lady comes close to Kasturi, saying "You are Kasturi, I have heard a lot about you. Manav always talks about you." She sits beside Manav and Kasturi too occupies her seat. "You see, for so many years, Manav had so many contacts from trust and politics, but he doesn't call anyone home. You are the first person among his official contacts who have come home. I have seen your DP on Whatsapp. You are very sweet, "Katuri smiles without uttering anything. They have a brief chat before Kasturi leaves. This visit only mentioned that she has to have a local there. He would have just mentioned it over the phone she thought.

After a lot of searching and a couple of rejections to match Manav's criteria for office space, finally Rakesh is able to finalise a small office after getting the go-ahead from Manav. It costs Kasturi two more visits and tons of patience.

Rakesh submits the agreement papers to Manav. The next few visits by Kasturi are just waiting for Manav to visit her office with his so-called officials for inspection. But no one turns up and the sequence of Manav calling her to Kolhapur, making her wait for 2-3 days, pretending to be busy and either not meeting or just talking on the phone continues. It has been few months now, and with the tight finances, it is becoming very difficult to pay the rent of that unutilized office. The only purpose served was that Kasturi could get freshened up there and had an option to pass time while waiting for Manav's call post working hours.

During this time, Rakesh is a great moral support for Kasturi, and she would visit his house for one meal at least whenever she visited Kolhapur. His family members would always extend their gratitude towards Kasturi and Avinash for training Rakesh and treating him just like family and not as an employee.

It is a reasonable deal that Kasturi finalise during this visit. They closed a deal for 8 machines, and this is a big relief in the financial crisis. They wait till late evening because Kasturi is keen on taking the purchase order herself, but for some reason not known to them, it doesn't happen. The purchase officer assures that Rakesh can collect it the next day. As usual, Kasturi visits Sai Baba Mandir and asks Rakesh to leave. She thanks and thanks to her Sai Baba for the deal but also argues about why her trust in Manav is not yet breaking, for despite trying hard why were orders not coming as before? She feels stuck. Feels like paving the wrong way.

The following day in the afternoon in Mumbai Kasturi is desperate to receive an order confirmation from Rakesh and calls him several times, but that day and another fortnight order is not issued at all despite Rakesh's visits to the hospital. Finally, Rakesh conveys to Kasturi that they lost the order to a competitor. This is more than a blow. Kasturi manages to hold onto Rakesh's morals and confidence yet again.

At this point, with so many visits and so many chats, Kasturi almost feels that probably all this so-called 'willing to solve your problems' approach was only to extract money from her situation. When she gave up on following him, he would regularly send 'Good Morning' messages. She was tired of all this.

Unexpectedly, Kasturi receives a message from Manav one afternoon "Your 180 machine order is confirmed and the agreement between Trust and your company is ready. Please come and collect it." She feels a sink in her heart, not believing it and just thinking of when he will end all this. She takes it as another lie. Not wanting to call on his bluff anymore, she just conveys to him that she is suffering from viral fever and is not in the position to travel.

Kasturi gives up on Manav's proposal, but he is not willing to give up on testing her patience yet.

A fortnight later they meet in the trust office at around 10.30am. Manav had mentioned that the agreement between the trust and her company for 180 machines was ready and she had to sign the same and could take one copy along. Rakesh drops Kasturi near the trust office before heading to attend a service call. A young office boy greets her wholeheartedly with an innocent smile, taking away a bit of stress from her.

She enters the cabin and before looking at Manav, notices two booklets kept on the table facing the side where Kasturi would sit. She occupies the chair greeting a hello. Not going formal, she picks up one booklet titled 'Agreement between the trust and her company in bold'. Manav takes another copy of the agreement and randomly turns pages, mentioning terms of the order, payments and execution.

Indeed, the agreement is there with the sign and seal of the trust, but Kasturi is still not able to accept that it is real. She surfs through pages, not reading the content but recollecting how Manav had managed to send her SMSs, which looked like from some banks during her loan matter or some Government portals after she paid cash to him. This is most likely the point at which she lost faith in Manav. These documents don't seem real to her though it appeared so. She wants to just wind up and leave. She continuously questions herself why she has even come there.

Kasturi is blunter than ever "Manav, this is fine, but what about our work for which we paid money? Moreover, we will not be able to pay anything for this order unless we get our payments. I know this order is big and capable of taking us out of the financial crisis, but we don't have anything." Manav sounding helpful mentions, "we will need to spend, but don't worry that we will pay in parts as we receive our payments." Katuri further says, "Yes, but even importing these many machines is not possible without advance." Manav senses something wrong and asks her if she is fine. "What is the matter? You look upset today." Kasturi is not able to hold on and tears flow from her eyes. She is not even willing to look at his face. She is just silent for some time. Manav raises his hand to place it over Kasturi's hand which she is resting on the booklet lying on the table. She simply pulls her hand back and points her other hand at Manav, suggesting; stop! She gets up from her place in a reflex action and sits again as Manav pulls his hand back. He is furious at her "See, you said you had started taking me to be a friend and I am not even able to console you." "Console me, really? You know very well how I managed to give you Rs.7lacs, when we had absolutely nothing. I have been following up with you for the past one and a half years. Sometimes you say we need to meet someone, sign some documents, go to some office, and someone will come to our office. But I've never seen that 'someone'. Now you put these papers in front of me and want me to still believe you that this is true?

There is a knock on the door and the office boy comes in reminding Manav "Sir, we need to leave. The meeting will start in 15 minutes." Kasturi is not bothered to even look at either of them while Manav says, "You wait, and I will be back in half an hour." Kasturi just sighs as he leaves. Settling down with her anger, she notices that these booklets are not to be seen on the table. She didn't even notice when and where he kept those copies while they talked. With a slow pace she picks up a glass of water and drinks it almost in a sip, followed by another glass.

She dials Rakesh's number, who already notices Manav leaving his office while waiting downstairs. They decide to leave his office and carry on with their appointments. Kasturi comes out of Manav's cabin. Manav's office boy enquires, "Madam, will you come back?" Sir asked you to wait. He will come in some time." Kasturi smiles at him and says, "We are just nearby. Call me once your sir is in the office, I'll come." She leaves with no hope that he will come back for the day.

To her surprise, Manav calls her and requests her to come to his office. He also mentions that he shall text address and he does. Kasturi asks Rakesh to check-up which this address is and Rakesh confirms "Madam this is his office, I have been there to give our office agreement copy and we went searching for him once there if you remember." They reach there at his specified time. The office boy informs them that

Manav is with Naik. Kasturi didn't expect that Naik existed. Manav comes out and tells her "You always thought that I took money from you and was bluffing right? Come and meet Naik he will tell you what the fact is." Kasturi follows Manav to his cabin. Manav pulls a chair for her. This guy Naik looks at Kasturi, she feels the poke of his look from his glasses. She looks at Manav and takes out her visiting card, hands over it to Naik introducing herself but he is not interested and that is so evitable from his face. He passes a weird smile looking at Manav then looks at Kasturi "I have got 4.35Cr sanctioned for you but what will you be able to give against that Madam?" Manav gets up from his seat "Dada I told you." Naik laughs loudly and shouts at Manav "You know I don't like it if anyone talks in between while I am talking, sit there." Kasturi has not seen this huge Manav with such a pitiful face before. Kasturi too shakes from within but manages to hide her fear as Naik continues "I can do anything on Manav's say you see. Now I understand why he didn't want me to meet you even when I asked several times." Manav again gets up, this time his face is red with anger. Kasturi looks at Manav holding tears in her eyes. She is all set to get up and leave. Naik calls the office boy "Get something for Madam." Manav says "She will not have anything dada. You were here so I called her to meet you." Naik takes out his visiting card and places it in front of Kasturi. Her watery eyes catch a glimpse of the logo on it and the rest appears hazy to her. Kasturi understands that this person is carrying wrong intentions as he further says "Money doesn't matter much to me, I have lots of money. I told Manav to let me meet madam and put my request, after all its give and take. What's wrong with that? Now, if I sanction 4-5 Crores for you I will also want something in return, right? Manav interrupts, raising his voice "dada!" He holds Kasturi's hand and pulls her out of the cabin. His hold is so tight that it leaves a mark on her wrist. He is furious at her "Happy?" Katuri frees her hand from Manav's with a jerk and just slaps him in an attempt to vent out. Surprisingly Manav's mother enters the office, she almost witnesses the slap or maybe not! She stands still guessing that something is wrong there. She looks at Manav with a question mark on her face. Manav too looks at her "You were to come here much early maa." Then looking at Kasturi he utters"I hope you understand why I was not wanting you to meet these people. But you don't trust me and had doubts about me so I had to call you here today as your amount and order is also sanctioned." Kasturi is all in tears by now. Rakesh keeps staring at both of them. Naik shouts from inside "Manav." Manav gets in the cabin. The loud noise of conversation is not very clear though. It sounds like some strong argument. Few words of Manav and Naik hit Kasturi's ears which are more than unpleasant. Manav shouts at the peak of his voice "Dada I said she is not that kind of female." Manav's mom's face turns red after hearing all this. She enters his cabin and then there is complete silence there. Kasturi looks at Rakesh breathing sharply. She runs out of Manav's office dragging herself on the black tarred road. She couldn't believe what she just witnessed. She walks till its dead end. Again gets scared, looks behind and finds Rakesh running towards her. He stands in front of her saying "Just wait madam; I will get my bike "she nods and takes her bag from him.

Her phone rings and its Avinash. She feels like running to him and hugging him tightly but, for now she is not even able to pick up his call and talk.

On the way back home Rakesh mentions it to her checking if she remembers it, that sometimes back when they were waiting for Manav and called him from outside the office. They figured out Manav from a distance but Manav had said he was out of town. Kasturi of course recollects this episode. Rakesh mentions that this same person was accompanying Manav at that time. Rakesh has seen him from a partial glass partition at Manav's office today.

She decides to stay at Rakesh's house that night. It is almost 10.30 pm and by the time they reach his house, everyone is asleep. Rakesh's wife Nupoor insists on having dinner but Kasturi just wants to lie down and close her eyes. Kasturi cries throughout the night. Checks her phone sometimes in the middle of the night and there are seven missed calls from Manav. She slides her phone under the mattress after sending a message to Avinash "missing you."

She is shattered. All hopes are buried. All this time she thought she was smartly dealing with Manav keeping his approach at the bay! At times she even accepted that maybe he likes me in a good sense, he may go out of the way and get this work done. But the picture she saw was not complete and there was a much ugly face to it, which Manav managed to hide from her throughout.

Analysing the sequence she also realises that Manav has purposefully called his mother to his office to avoid all that which couldn't be avoided though.

She recollects all her visits throughout the night. Those words in Manav's cabin repeated several times. She could hardly sleep that night. She had hoped that these follow-ups will lead to some solution that could get her and all those trusted her out of the financial crisis. Probably, all this was not for sailing her through but to make her learn some lessons, lessons for paving a rough path, probably a wrong path.

A Sharp ring breaks her sleep and she receives a call before opening her eyes. "Kasturi, where are you? I want to meet you. I will come wherever you are." She disconnects Manav's call. He calls again. She switches off her phone and gets ready. She visits the owner of her rented office along with Rakesh and calls off the agreement. Rakesh has no questions for her. He just follows whatever she does.

How coud she leave without an argument with her Sai? She questions and questions! Replies to her questions are to be found out by her.

Just before her train Manav calls again. She receives this time "I am done with this option Manav. I don't need that money." Manav tries hard to prove his innocence and he keeps on talking and explaining to her how these people are and that he will take care of

Naik. The worst is done and she need not worry. There is no need to deny the amount and that he can still fix it up for her." Kasturi just says one sentence before disconnecting "If this is how it is Manav, who will trust me for getting this money without compromising just because you safeguarded."

Now, she doesn't even want to argue with Manav. She prefers to maintain her silence while he does his bit of convincing. Her thoughts run through lots of ifs and buts. Kasturi calls Sheela telling her that this option cannot be worked out. Sheela senses a sense of 'feeling low' in her voice. She talks to her for quite some time regarding other irrelevant topics to make her feel at ease till Kasturi sounds better. Sheela is well aware that her negligence has put Kasturi in this situation and Kasturi has not even confronted her. She just accepted Sheela's mistake and took over the responsibility towards one and all involved.

That night when Manav called with the so-called intention of helping her, pouring all information showing that he cared; he probably had his thorough homework and was lucky enough to find Kasturi in this problem. Manav's words poke in her ears.

"Who is Sheela?" What is Femys Creations? How are you involved?
"Your company no more exists; the entire warehouse was on fire a day before the consignment was to be dispatched. Your friend for whatever reason failed to get the insurance in time and lost everything. She managed to borrow the money with the help of your CA and her other contacts and has been paying you for

a few months. But this will not continue further as not only she but the company is also in heavy debts. Craftsmen are looking forward to their payments which they may never receive. Along with the consignment, the property you bought for this work is also burnt to ashes." For Months Manav keeps posting her thoughtful good morning and good night messages till it is time from his side to wave goodbye.

Sing like no one is listening

She runs out of the elevator to her doorway, and ding ding…, ding ding her finger reflects the restlessness in her body accompanying her voice, "opeeeeeen…, quick." Her elder son opens up questioning "what?" She gives an indicative smile at Akshay and he reacts, "oh ha, today is your singing class audition for the program "he continues, "Please, please, mom let me join you." She lifts Akshay gasping, "see I can no longer hold you, you are a grownup boy now so, you understand that you can't join" Akshay hugs her tightly in no mood to agree but eventually has to.

Finishing her cooking quickly she makes Varun ready and leaves with him waving at Akshay and Avinash. Avinash shouts from behind "I will pick you both." She runs to Avinash, hugs him saying "Love you" and rushes.

Dropping Varun at his dance class she runs to the adjacent building and stops near the entrance, glances inside. Her heartbeat has a higher pace than normal now. She slowly enters the room leaving all her hurry outside. Looking around she spots Sheela in the audience and slowly waves at her slightly showing that she is worried. Sheela raises both thumbs ups trying to say "you will do it."

Looking at the musicians she always gets goosebumps and today is no exception. She joins fellow singers.

Auditions begin and she recollects her past few sessions.

A middle aged joining any activity is taken up as a pass-time activity by most and this was what exactly happened with Kasturi as well. After lots of search, she figures out this singing class but was not happy about the approach of the teacher, not only towards her but towards other students as well. Teaching is so mechanical and she could sense those soulless practice sessions. Some kids used to come just because parents want them to learn to sing; 'an Indian Idol' syndrome or whatever.

But, neglecting all this negative side she tries to concentrate only on her practice, take guidance and proceed. While she had joined to learn semi-classical, by this time she had convinced herself that whatever the teacher says is to be followed. Not happy with the songs they choose for her though.

Her turn arrives and she misses hearing her name, repetition of her name's announcements only brings her back to the present time. She looks at Sheela as she walks toward the microphone. The grip of it is slippery as her palm sweat in anxiety. Auditions, class, auditorium nothing mattered to her. What mattered was the microphone in her hands, musicians matching her scale. She was singing in front of the audience.

She picks up with a sigh and there is pin-drop silence in the hall. She feels words flow effortlessly. Her stage fright and anxiety is overshadowed by soothing feelings in her heart and mind. Continuing, she opens her eyes gazing at the harmonium player who nods at her for being on the correct scale and she notices people walking outside the hall coming inside to listen to her. A slight smile of satisfaction prints on her lips as she concludes. There is continuous clap for more than 3-4mins and she is overwhelmed. She feels happy about her song selection. She looks at her teacher who ignores her as usual, which she never understands "why?"

The next day is the day of her first-time performance; she is expecting her family members who are equally excited to see her on stage. All set behind the curtain. Kasturi peeps out at the audience and spots her kids looking at her.

Curtain is about to rise when her teacher approaches her and mentions that the song which Kasturi sang in Audition was given to some other girl and Kasturi was given some different song that she had never practised. She is like "Madam, I have never practised this song." Her teacher is in no mood to listen to what Kasturi had to say. Moreover, this is a sensual song and Kasturi had never attempted this.

This was what her teacher did ever since Kasturi had refused to take up private classes paying heavy fees. Her teacher learned she was an entrepreneur and expected her to spend on private classes. On the contrary, Kasturi enjoyed being with fellow students. Young boys and girls and their temperaments attracted her and she enjoyed their company.

Kasturi reaches out to her mom in the audience. Akshay immediately jumps towards her while Varun looks at her in the expectation that she will hold him but she just sits beside her mother saying "actually I don't want to sing today, I am …" her mother asks "what's the matter? Don't want to sing means something serious. What is it?" Tears roll down as she speaks, " Madam has given my song to someone else and I have been given a song which I have never tried and it is such that I can't sing in front of you" she continues "let's go, anyways I wanted to leave this class, be it so." Her Mom holds her hand with a smile on her face "I know you are not a professional singer but art is worship and do not deny any chance to worship your passion. Just think of the original singer, don't recollect the on-screen visuals, just recollect how she is calm and composed while singing this song on stage." Kasturi is still not in agreement and argues "I will not be able to justify this song as I have never attempted it", Her mom reminds her, "how many times you have listened to it since you were young? It is already there in your mind. You just need to open the treasure box and I am sure you will perform well." Kasturi look at Akshay who was witnessing this with the hope that her mom doesn't give up. She gently hugs Akshay and kisses Varun's forehead before approaching backstage.

While the program proceeds Kasturi prepares herself to accept and believe what her mom explained. It is her turn on stage and she walks toward the mic. Looking at the audience is a never-before experience for her. She is holding her passion tight in her heart and sighs before she hears the first chord. She is not aware of how the song flows; she just sings and opens her eyes when the audience shouts once more, once more. She finds it difficult to believe this response from the audience and she realises that she had thoroughly enjoyed singing this song as well. She looks at her mom and passes a flying kiss with wet eyes.

Her teacher approaches her saying "only your song got once more, good", these words no longer soothe Kasturi though she bows down to touch her teacher's feet seeking her blessings.

 She discontinues this class with a heavy heart. But, for Varun and Akshay their mom is a star now and a singer forever.

It is a small thing in a bigger picture maybe but that is what life is all about. We plan for something, we desire for something but something else is served on our plate and not just that, we are to even witness our desire on someone else's plate. We have to deal with this. We need to accept and consume what is served. This small episode teaches Kasturi to face whatever comes in our way and still perform with fair justice. Deep down it gets registered and pops up in life when needed.

Whenever she notice an advertisement for the singing classes her heart bounced a bit extra and she remembered how she was treated last time, a bitter experience could not calm her thirst though. She again gets attracted to one such class where the teacher seemed to be polite and with a pleasant personality.

So, her second attempt to learn what she loved

begins.

She again joins a general class, where 8-10 females of her age and few may be a little more aged mixed up very well. Kasturi is more than happy to be part of them. They all liked her and so did she. Singing behind the teacher in the chorus is an altogether different feeling than learning alone. She thoroughly enjoys it.

Though struggling with the finances, this hour of the day while she practised her singing lessons is always what she looked forward to, and forget all that she is to address the very next moment after that hour.

Days pass and it doesn't take long for Kasturi to understand that this teacher always compares Kasturi with herself for no reason. She finds it silly when her teacher says "we look the same from Behind" and it shocks Kasturi when during one household function at the teacher's place she asks Kasturi to change her dress and wear one of the teacher's dresses. Her teacher is happy to see that it fit Kasturi and never bothered that it made Kasturi so uncomfortable.

All the students of her batch are supposed to sing one song on this occasion not deliberately but by mistake the teacher forgets to present Kasturi. By this time all the praises like "You would have easily become a playback singer, had you taken your singing seriously and in time, your voice is very sweet" turns to "I have been singing since I was 3 years old and how can you be a good singer when you start learning at 42."

It is Kasturi's first exam ever and she is excited and anxious as well. They have had practice sessions though but exams are exams. To present in front of unknown experts gives her a bouncing ball feelings in stomach.

She enters while all her co-students are already there. The tabla player is fixing the notes and her teacher is on Harmonium. Kasturi quickly approaches her teacher, touching her feet and seeking blessing just to hear "perform well, my prestige is at stake." Kasturi just looks at her passing a smile and occupies her place.

Arriving almost 20mins late and then having tea time at the beginning delays the exam time by almost 45mins.

Kasturi's heartbeat starts pounding with the beginning of the harmonium. Tests began. Kasturi's turn lands up with her chance to pick-up from 'Pa' and complete the swarnamala (*Octav*). The second round is a question-answer session to know about the basics. The question comes from the examiner "which side of the singer is taal (*rhythm*) instrument placed and soor (*tune*) placed?" Kasturi is the only one raising their hand for this and quickly replies "Soor on the left and taal on the right." Examiner is happy about this reply. Next is actual singing and Kasturi is more excited for this round. She begins at her turn and completes the 'Mukhda' as decided. Examiner stops her in-between "continue till next two lines after Mukhda and she does so before relaxing.

Examiner looks at her teacher explaining "her higher note was so perfect so I wanted to hear if she goes down too correctly" teacher nods with acceptance of his opinion. Kasturi couldn't stop herself from asking, "was it ok sir?" and he just smiles.

Everything looked fine with this class but Kasturi failed to understand what type of complex came in between.

Kasturi enters her regular class and sits passing a smile at her friend. The teacher starts laughing, suddenly seeking everyone's attention and saying "You know everyone has one soor but Kasturi is so special she has two soor (which meant, out of tune). It pokes deep down and Kasturi is on the verge of crying. Her friend places her hand on Kasturi's hand expressing her to be calm but everyone notices droplets at the edge of her eyes. No one utters a word and class continues.

Back home Kasturi and her friend discuss probably the teacher being unhappy that she is not taking the private class and also the topic of the teacher's paralyzed husband and her emotional status doesn't go untouched. They conclude that let both of them together try a private class and see if things improve. Kasturi is so possessed by learning music that she is willing to take yet another chance. It takes quite a bit of time for them to convince their teacher that they want to come for private tuition but both together. Unwillingly, the teacher agrees.

Few classes go on smoothly but soon it gets

converted into just attendance and the teacher would do her household work or show them old photo albums etc most of the times.

It is time for one small program and everyone is given one song to perform at the event. Kasturi is willing to learn and present one song she always liked. But her suggestion only yields a comment "You will take 10years to learn this and still you won't be able to sing it correctly" Kasturi's heart sinks once again but she doesn't give up. She practises and to her surprise at the last moment as Kasturi occupies her seat in front of the mic, with a pleasant face her teacher mentions some other song while announcing Kasturi's name. Kasturi looks at her teacher who just walks away from the stage after announcing. Kasturi takes one deep breath and remembers her mother's face and she could hear "wah " in-between as she continues. She gets praise from the audience and many approach her enquiring if she will sing at some of their functions. While she is surrounded by many, her eyes try to locate her teacher who is just ignoring all this.

Few classes continue though. Kasturi understands that this is not what she was looking for and finally gives up on this class too.

For months Kasturi just puts ON her Tabla and Tanpura machine and listens but couldn't sing at all.

Her friend keeps on calling and convincing her that it was just a bad experience and that she should not give up on singing but Kasturi knows now that her teachers couldn't understand her passion and thirst.

She feels if it was her faith to learn she would have got some good teachers and all this would not happen.

She concludes that learning to sing was not meant for her.

Months pass while she is still struggling with her mental status due to challenges on the personal and professional front. Her passion for singing always proved to be a saviour in disguise not only once but several times throughout her rough phase.

Ganesh festival is round the corner and it so happens that her close friends suggest that they form a group and present a small program on one of the evenings during the festival. Kasturi thoroughly enjoys the whole process for almost three months where they all meet every evening for practice. Each one suggests songs and they land up presenting a program of devotional songs in Marathi, Hindi, Gujarathi, and Tamil.

Her friend from the singing class is finally able to convince her to join another singing class. The teacher is male, and considering her experience Kasturi is a little reluctant to decide to join but finally she gets focused on fulfilling her urge from within.

This is too true to believe that she is learning like never before. This teacher picks the flaws of his students and worked on them. In a short period, Kasturi is able to sing classical to some extent and she finally looks forward to going much further in her passion.

The whole of the week Kasturi would look forward to Monday mornings. She would meet her friend at the centre point and they both took an autorickshaw from there to the class. Their discussion would only be about how lucky they are to finally land up joining this class. This friend is a retired female who used to enjoy Kasturi's company and always praised her for managing her home, business and then taking out time for her passion.

Kasturi is more than happy when sir involves her in organising their programs. He requests her to visit an auditorium with him which needs to be finalised for their program.

She meets her sir directly at the auditorium and they reach the office. As decided, Kasturi led the discussion for fixing the date, time slot, and final negotiation too. Out of the auditorium, sir expresses his gratitude and also mentions that she can take charge of organising all further programs as that is not his cup of tea.

Taking out time from her busy schedule is not difficult as she already started planning how she would perceive her passion further. She enjoys organising and plans further to form a Music company with all this experience and gives a chance for newcomers to use that platform, organising such shows.

Program day arrives and it is a beautiful ambiance. All

her co-students are in pretty and colourful saris and male singers in kurtas as pre-decided. Some are arranging the placement of instruments, some looking after flower decorations, drinks to be served to the guests, and the sitting arrangements. Every part of that hall is getting ready to flow with the music.

This time on the stage is much more relaxed for Kasturi as the practice is thoroughly done. Completing her part of Raag Khamaj gives her immense satisfaction like never before. She gets engrossed in music, and taking out time regularly for practice becomes a wanted challenge for her.

It is a Diwali night and Kasturi reaches home late at night after a family get-together at her brother's place. After a quick wash and putting both the kids to sleep she put her phone on charging as the battery is drained by now. She switches it on and there is this continuous beep of messages pouring like anything. It is her sir, so many messages!!

"Why are you not replying?" "Why is your phone off?" and it continues and continues. She is scared at first and looking at the rest of the messages she realises things were not pleasant. Messages mention "you are looking so beautiful in this sari. I want to talk to you right now", and "I want to see you smile, Listen to your laughter right now." Kasturi just sits on her bed in shock. She falls short of expression; she looks at her Kids and just lies down next to Avinash holding his hand. She doesn't even bother that the phone is hanging attached to the charger without any support.

All her singing sessions run through. Her daily Monday routine, how decently sir would treat everyone, how respectfully he talked to one and all. She failed to understand what she had just seen on her phone screen. She keeps watching her phone but doesn't feel like touching it.

Her dream is hammered yet again and this time like never before. There is no going back. There is no explanation needed for these messages and she doesn't seek one either. She doesn't even feel like crying, her eyes are just wide open throughout the night.

There is no second thought that all she planned was just killed by a wild mind. She thinks, why me? What was I asking for? Was I dreaming about becoming a big professional singer? I just wanted to pursue my hobby, my passion on this small scale. She couldn't stop blaming her faith, finally saying to her Saibaba "you think I will be a big singer if I get a good teacher and hence you land me in some of the other issues whenever I try." Her thoughts continue. This time she is angry rather than being sad. She thinks she would never see his face again.

The next day is Monday and as the phone ring at 8.30am Kasturi knew who it was, her friend was waiting at their designated spot for her. Kasturi conveys "you proceed and I will join a bit late." Kasturi gets ready and reaches the doorstep of her class 15mins late. Sir is normal with a pleasant face as always and utters "how come late today? Come sit, we will complete 'Malkauns' Aaroha today. Her eyes are burning with anger as she looks directly into his eyes. He is still calm. Session complete and they leave. She walks with her friend, she is quiet, analysing how a person can have two faces. Never had she experienced an odd look from him, not even today. Is he the same person? She thinks and more thoughts gather till her friend interrupts "What is the problem? Why are you so quiet today? Kasturi blabbers "I just wanted to see his face if it has any guilt or something but he is so normal as if he did nothing wrong." Kasturi's friend is not able to understand what she was talking about and asks "wrong, what wrong?" "Yes, everything is wrong, what we see, what we hear, what we understand can be so different from reality. You see a different picture altogether and the real picture is so different." Kasturi's friend fails to understand but just gives her space not to enquire too much and waves a bye for the day.

Just before reaching home, Kasturi's phone rings and she picks to know what he has to say now. Her face emits unpleasant expressions to hear her sir's voice and is not shocked to hear "Just forget everything, continue class. We will continue learning and singing." Probably, sir sensed that she won't continue for sure. Kasturi replies before hanging up "You were my Guru and you have dishonoured your position" and she hangs up.

End of another Chapter of an attempt for her. She is sad of course but continues with her one-hour daily practice and each practice rolls those committed and pure learning sessions she experienced with her sir. Even today Kasturi is not able to believe those messages and takes it as a bad dream.

She continues practising songs, singing, recording, and listening for herself.

For years together she had this habit of recording her songs and sharing them with her friends. She continues that and her heart fills with these tiny praises. Days fly, and so does Kasturi's dream of genuinely learning to sing. The thought that it is not meant for her is seconded by many such episodes.

It is mid-winter and she notices chats in her school group. Few of them staying abroad were visiting India and there is this talk of reunion. She is happy about it and responds as "IN." Not very known in the group though, few of her close friends have personal chats fixing up dress code, etc. Not suggesting much, she agrees to whatever they decide.

They arrive and the venue is ready to witness the anxious, surprised, eager youngsters in their 40s. Unlike current days Kasturi used to be an introvert during school days. Still wishing many, she occupies a corner seat near her friends. There is a lot of noise out of excitement and a lot of energy in the room.

There is a Karaoke set up and everyone is enjoying it. Like everyone else Kasturi too is lost in this world taking time out from her present world. Suddenly she notices her friend Suchitra running towards the mic and unexpectedly she announces "friends, let's invite Kasturi for a song" and Kasturi loses a heartbeat. Not able to sing in front of this crowd, she hesitates and denies it. Suchitra pulls her and hands over the mic to her "I saw your post on Facebook, I know you sing." She is holding the mic after all her previous encounters not only for the first time but after 2-3 years altogether. She begins and with just the first word of the song the entire crowd shouts with excitement. She pauses, with a raised heartbeat and a slight smile on her face she finds herself lost in the song. She ends and there is complete silence in the room for a while before they explode with claps and shouts and all her friends run towards her and all of them surround her showering lots and lots of flowers of praise. All were surprised to hear her sing as no one knew about this. Many approach her asking "which division were you, I have never seen you." One shy girl whom not many knew was suddenly the talk of the event. What she felt about all this is beyond expressions.

That evening post the reunion, their group is full of chats about her song, recorded version is played again and again and some comments like "My entire family is your fan after they heard your song", "My daughter is been playing your song repeatedly since I am back home."Kasturi feels like a star as seen in movies like someone turns into a star overnight. She opens her bedroom window and feels the cool breeze waiting for her. Looking at the beautiful skyline of Mumbai she feels that this entire world is praising her and enjoying her song.

What was lost in every attempt to be a learned singer was found here! This one episode erased all bad feelings her learning experiences gave which she would never forget but it doesn't bother her anymore. Now, she no longer needs any certificate from anyone else, she is not bothered if someone is checking her 'notes' and she is not bothered if anyone is witnessing her singing.

That's how it is, all about your inner satisfaction. Once your heart is filled with satisfaction there is no space for discouragements. It doesn't matter how you sing, it only matters that you sing despite all odds. Life is a tune played for you and to catch the notes and flow with it gives life a true meaning, a true essence. Everyone may not be a perfect singer for the spectators but one should always sing like no one is listening and dance like no one is watching, only then it will be enjoyable and from the heart for the heart.

Kasturi is blessed to get the opportunity to be part of an event where one of her friends offers her to present two songs on Saibaba and where else but at Dwarka Mai at Shirdi. What can anyone like her ask for? It is not only a priceless offer from a friend but also a blessing from her Sai, she feels. Not only her vocal cords but every part of her body emits the feeling as she sings with the goose-bumps accompanying her till the end.

She gets another opportunity to be a part of this friend's troop who performs at Dandiya Nights at Mumbai's prestigious venue. It is tough to manage practice session and her physique gave up at times when she has to travel almost 2hrs one way after managing her household and work commitments but that is what passion is all about. She sings even Gujarathi songs and enjoys the moment thoroughly.

She is performing on stage. Her eyes catch a glimpse of her brother along with the rest of her family. Tiny droplets in his eye while watching her on stage doesn't go unnoticed by Kasturi.

Counter Measures

With insufficient funds for importing machines and still hoping not to give up, Kasturi keeps on calculating days and months wherein she has to hold-on, and probably something may work out and things get streamlined.

Finding no other way Kasturi refers to the list of payment defaulters and zeros down to two of them who have been using the machines and always giving some or the other excuse for not being able to pay.

Kasturi follows up rigorously with both of them. Rakesh visits Sangamner where a local NGO had made arrangements with their company for paying on a monthly basis with the assurance of a fair amount to be paid monthly. It is been 5-6months since the installation but there is no payment from the hospital. Moreover, Rakesh informs that the machines are not even being used. It is not only machines but the entire setup installed by the company including AC, water treatment plant to even a weighing machine. The doctor is just not able to get the patients. The entire setup is lying without benefit to anyone. The doctor is neither willing to pay nor return the machines.

Kasturi takes a stand. She calls Dr.Rane who is running this hospital and requests to return the machines. As expected he makes lots of excuses like "I have given an appointment to patients, a

Nephrologist will be joining soon and patients will follow then, some inspection of the hospital and what not. As for Kasturi, she knew it would not be easy to get the machines back. She contacts the trustees and explains her situation. They take it seriously mainly as they feel it to be their responsibility to help her out with getting machines back as they were lying idol.

Trustees take a couple of days to try and convince the doctor to cooperate and either pay or return the machines and they too get the same excuses from him.

Kasturi sounds desperate talking to the trustee to help her out. Trustees ask her if she can visit Sangamner on Sunday as they have a monthly meeting and many of the trustees would be present. He also suggests that we can request the Chairman to accompany us and talk to the doctor in person. It is decided mutually that the doctor should not be aware of this and should come to him as a surprise.

A night before leaving for Sangamner, Kasturi keeps on thinking about all possibilities of the outcome. One thing she is sure of is that by hook or by crook she is settling the matter tomorrow. Her ticket is booked but something comes to her mind and at the last moment she cancels it. Not happy with the refund for cancellation but ignores her not-so-good feeling about this for now.

Kasturi picks up her phone and calls her regular delivery guy. He is surprised as he receives her call at 11 pm. "How come so late Madam?" he sounds not only sleepy but even drunk.. Kasturi enquires, "Ganesh, are you again drunk?"Ganesh defends himself "No madam, after your scolding I am not drinking" He understands there is no way he can fool her so admits "Just sometimes madam, tomorrow is sunday and so no work and I can get up a little late."

 Kasturi comes to the point "we have to go to Sangamner tomorrow morning." He asks "How many machines madam? What time should I come to the office?" Kasturi briefs him "no, tomorrow we need to go and pick up machines from that Hospital." She reminds him about the delivery of these machines 6-7 months ago and he recollects. He is in the full mood for further discussion but Kasturi hangs up saying that she will meet him at toll point and explain further while on the way.

Whenever she travelled her journey used to be her absolute 'ME time'. She would not be angry, furious, sad, or extra happy depending on her meeting or would be meetings. Throughout her journey, she would live to its fullest.

As Ganesh had nicely from Kasturi for drinking last night, he tries to please her by suggesting a dhaba for lunch. Dhaba-style eggplant serving is just too good.

It is before the decided time, Kasturi enters the corridor of the trustee's house. He is ready with his team and without wasting time in any discussions they all leave. Kasturi had instructed Ganesh to wait a little far from the hospital as she had not mentioned to anyone that she had come with so much preparation.

Trustees enter the hospital. The receptionist and other staff welcome them. Dr.Rane is not in the hospital. The trustee calls him up "we just had a meeting today and after that, we thought we could visit the hospital and spend some time with you discussing expansion plans. We are in your cabin, come as soon as possible." The trustee requests Kasturi to just be calm and patient while they would talk to Dr.Rane.

It is 3pm by now, a good time for Dr.Rane to relax on this Sunday afternoon. He has no choice but to be there within 20mins. He enters the cabin and his face turns pale seeing Kasturi. That is the least he expects. The chairman of the hospital accompanies by senior trustees takes his breath away. The first thing he does after occupying his seat is, take a couple of sips from the glass of water placed on the table without even noticing that it was placed in front of the chairman.

Now, looking at Kasturi right in front of him unexpectedly bothers him. Without anyone saying or asking anything to him Dr.Rane starts on his own "Good that madam is also here so now in front of all of you i repeat that once my inspection is done I will return machines to her."

Dr.Rane is made to understand that he has no option but to return the machines which he agrees without argument but insisted that he will return after 15days once his inspection is over. There is quite a bit of heated discussions wherein trustees take up a few other matters with Dr.Rane which is irrelevant to

Kasturi. She chooses to be calm and patient and just prayed that her decision to get the tempo along should not prove wrong. When Avinash opposed her for doing so she only argued that if she can get the machines then she would face difficulty arranging transport as she is travelling on Sunday.

Kasturi keeps witnessing their altercations, closing her eyes. Suddenly she gets up looking at the Chairman; she almost shouts "sir." Pin drop silence follows in the cabin. Lowering her tone she puts up straight "Sir, I want my machines back today itself and I won't go back without them." Dr.Rane too gets up. His inertia to argue still exists. Taking advantage of other topics he tries to divert the machine's topic. Chairman gets up from his seat and heads toward Dr.Rane. Holding both his shoulders he makes him sit on his chair. Force applied on Dr.Rane's shoulders is quite evitable to all present there. Chairman warns him "enough of your excuses. Madam is taking machines today; that's it." Not waiting for anyone else's reaction, Kasturi comes out of the cabin after conveying a quick thanks to the trustees, "Thank you sir, it means a lot."

Kasturi calls Ganesh immediately who is at the Hospital in no time. Kasturi disconnects both the machines and guides Ganesh to take out ACs and all other big and small equipment belonging to them. With the help of a couple of ward boys, everything is loaded in the tempo and fastened thoroughly by thick robs.

The first thing Kasturi does is call Avinash who teases

her to be a 'Rani of Jhansi'.

Kasturi carries out a few more such operations and recovers 7 machines from the customers who had not paid a penny for their sweet reasons. At couple of places she does fail and as Avinash suggests, opts for concentrating on more orders rather than approaching any authorities for recovery.

Her follow-ups with other trusts and NGOs for her project continue along with the regular follow-ups. Challenge now is not getting orders alone, but getting funds as well which would support her project of Haemodialysis units in the rural sector.

The Good Morning Friends

Kasturi keeps surfing on the internet throughout the days, making a list of many companies who would be prospective donors from their Corporate Social Responsibilities (CSR) funds.

Taking guidance from Dr.Inamdar, Director of the Trust for whom Manav worked for. She approaches many such Top companies. The idea is machines donated by the company/donor to the trust who can in turn use them for underprivileged patients. Since being referred by Dr.Inamdaar she is well treated but that's not all she was looking for. Each meeting and each follow-up are just enough to make her comfortable for the next follow-up and nothing more than that.

One Saturday afternoon while returning from one of such meetings she receives a call and she picks up the unknown number flashing on her phone.

Hello!" she utters softly. "Hello, I am Prabhu I met you at Dr.Inamdaar's office some time back." Kasturi is surprised. It is from Prabhu, from office of one of the ministers. She recollects meeting him with Dr.Inamdaar but she didn't expect him to call her. Another light of hope pops up as she is not personally known to him and he was not expected to have her contact number.

"Can you meet me tomorrow in Pune? I will be visiting one of my relatives. If you can give me one hard copy of your Haemodialysis unit project, I have talked to one NGO who can help you in this" he briefs. "Yes sir Sure" Kasturi replies with gratitude.

Prabhu shares his address. Kasturi opts to take an early morning train to Pune. As usual, she is not able to have a sound sleep even that night. It is all about her thoughts; he called so probably he is serious. He must have taken my number from Dr.Inamdar so there must be something positive this time and she gets many such thoughts before she gets up, gets ready, and boards the train.

Her head is heavy and she is having a nauseatic feeling continuously. Normally she is happy to have a window seat but today she requests a fellow passenger for an exchange of seats as she feels severe nausea and feels may have to visit the restroom. Leaning her head on the headrest, she keep her eyes close. She tries to relax. Nausea just gets severe and she almost runs to the restroom. She feels better after puking but is still not comfortable. She holds her bag pack and tries to rest for a while. She wants to go back home to her kids and relax but has to convince herself that it is just one meeting and hopefully things may work out this time.

Kasturi gets down at Pune station. Slowly moving with the crowd climbing the bridge she notices a very old woman sitting helplessly for someone could be generous and give her a penny or two serving her at least something to eat. It is very difficult for Kasturi to just pass by such people. Even if she is in a hurry she would buy some eatables and give them. But today she is feeling so uneasy that she hardly feels like going to the nearby stall to buy anything and give it to this lady. She opts to at least give her some money. Standing in front of this lady stretching her eyelids of tired eyes, Kasturi opens her bag to reach out for her money purse. She is not able to find it. Searches for that in another compartment of her bag but is again not able to find it. She gets anxious over it when she is not able to find it at all. The old lady keeps looking up at Kasturi with hope and Kasturi is on the verge of tears. She spots a bench and sits trying to calm herself. Again opens her bag thoroughly searching for her money purse and realises that it is not there. Taking no time further she calls Avinash asking if she forgot it at home. She sounds like crying. "Just see if my money purse I left-back." Avinash knows how she is, he makes an unsuccessful attempt to calm her down "I will look for it and call back, don't worry and don't cry."

Kasturi is restless and without waiting for Avinash's call she calls him in just 5mins. Avinash doesn't receive. She disconnects but keeps staring at it and getting more restless. Avinash calls and she picks up instantly. It is all about more tears now. She hangs up. She starts analysing and understanding why her fellow passenger was so quick to just get out of the compartment and almost disappear in the crowd.

Kasturi looks at the old lady whose gaze is still on her.

This time she was carrying more cash than ever. This was the first time she lost something in such a small Journey and this comparatively such a small amount meant so much more today.

That feeling of giving hope to the old lady and now left with nothing to fulfil makes Kasturi's heart sink. People close to Kasturi knew she would shed tears for small matters but only she knows the deep unpleasant feeling of a breaking hope.

Lodging a police complaint with Railway police kills more than an hour, delay's her meeting, and cancels her visit to her friends.

She reaches the address and finds it strange for Prabhu had mentioned that he is visiting his relatives but it was his own house, his own family, his wife, and his granddaughter. Kasturi hands over the project report to Prabhu and briefs about the same. Assurance from him that he will get this done sums-up their meeting.

Several follow ups from Kasturi but Prabhu turn out to be just another contact to the list she is following up for her project.

Its visit to Kolhapur for Dr.Kamat's unit is at the final stage. Dr.Inamdaar suggested she meet Chougule the Director of an NGO saying they have huge funds and the other day he mentioned to Dr.Inamdar about their interest in health care. Kasturi makes a casual visit to Chaugule. Kasturi feels his calm and composed personality very pleasant. He mentions everything about his NGO and its operations. Their donations go for books and fees and meals for underprivileged kids. He also mentions that he is also planning to donate to health care. She is happy to hear that. But that is not all in this meeting.

Kasturi after handing over her proposal gets up saying "looking forward to working on the project sir." Chaugule laughs and replies "yes of course, and also look forward to my Good morning messages at 5am daily." Kasturi smiles in response.

On the way back she realises all these big shots and CEOs and Directors were so very good to talk to and treated her well but nothing more than 'a Good morning friend'. She has been receiving good morning messages from many of them and nothing more than that. That one message that her project is considered is still a distant hope.

Missing beats of two hearts

Both Kasturi and Avinash continue approaching many companies for seeking their distribution. Hard luck continues to be at her back.

Kasturi never missed the opportunities to accomplish some of her interests from situations when business meetings didn't click but still she fetched her Interest out of it. A visit to the holy Shrine Vaishnodevi was one such encounter. She visited the place as an extension to her business meeting in Delhi. The alliance of the two companies lived short but this visit gave her a lifetime experience.

She has strong faith in the Goddess. It is said that you cannot plan for such holy visits rather the universe plans for you if you are to visit such places. It is not an easy trek and visiting the place all alone is no less than a challenge. It didn't seem to Kasturi though.

Many of the visits for exploring business opportunities eventually landed up in exploring nature, travel, and the people. Exploring life and its worth and much more than business and also saved her from getting frustrated at times.

Raj, one of their ex-colleague responds to Kasturi's message only for her to know that he too has been sailing the rough sea and is returning to India after a hardship of almost 5-6years in Kuwait. She is disheartened to know that he has lost all that he earned there in some business as his partner ditched him and he could only recover the amount from his partner sufficient to return and start something of his own in Kerala.

Before returning Raj was in talks with some company in Bangalore. At Kasturi's request, Raj proposed to the company to consider Kasturi's firm for distribution in Western India.

The primary discussion looked promising and was to be followed by 2 days of training in Bangalore. Raj was super excited to meet both his seniors. Being always thankful to Avinash for guiding and helping him get through his first job even after a rejection from the General Manager of the company in favour of his own candidate Raj spoke to Kasturi or Avinash just to mention how eager he is to meet them. By now all the attempts Kasturi made didn't yield any result and Avinash looked at this opportunity to be similar. Not very keen on both attending the training, Avinash finally agrees for it on Raj's pursuit. Kasturi misses a heartbeat to see their tickets of Udyan Express.

They board the train at Thane station. Unlike many of their previous travels, this one is overshadowed by all the tensions that prevailed through the years now. Sitting opposite each other occupying both window seats, Kasturi is not able to lift her head in an attempt to hide her tears, almost ready to spill off. Avinash is engaged in his laptop.

Kasturi notices herself sitting close to Avinash holding his hand. Kasturi looks beautiful in her plain wine-colored attire. Her hairs are dark brown with natural burgundy shine entangled in her pony. Her beautiful eyes full of dreams about the future appeared more talkative than her and her smile, as pure as it can be. Wrinkles of tension and thin hairline were missing then. Avinash is not willing to leave her hand, she pinches him taking care that fellow passengers do not notice and they laughed and laughed.

They wanted to forget the world and get lost in each other's arms but just smile at each other as Avinash kiss her forehead and stood near her middle berth holding her hand.

Kasturi watched herself and Avinash till she occupied her middle berth looking at Avinash who was already fast asleep before she could come back from the restroom. She replies to Raj's message before switching her phone to flight mode and posts him their hotel details.

Early morning at Banglore station and to their hotel is a short walk. Raj was to reach Bangalore by afternoon. They have a brief introductory session with Shivsagar, technical director of the company. Where Avinash senses that he is not willing to consider as they have no experience in this particular product range Kasturi is still positive.

Not only Raj but even Kasturi and Avinash get sentimental to meet each other after almost a decade and a half. Lunch at the nearby restaurants is full of their memories while Shivsagar has no option but to join their giggles throughout. Winding up the day

Shivsagar puts it up to Raj exactly what Avinash guessed. Kasturi is furious at Shivsagar as he would have mentioned this prior and not invited them for training. Raj too rejects their distribution for Kerala looking at their unprofessional approach. More than them Raj takes it to heart that he was coordinating and he felt like ditched by Shivsagar. They had their respective trains the next day and though Shivsagar insists that they all meet the next day again they opt for a Goodbye right across.

They have their few more ex-colleagues in Bangalore and Raj fix-ups a quick plan to have a small get-together for the next day across the lunch and where else but at the canteen of the hospital just for recreating the old memoirs.

It is just 5.30 pm as they walk out of the canteen. Avinash proposes to walk down to the nearest railway station rather than taking a cab. Kasturi instantly agrees, for she is always looking forward to walking along the roadside with Avinash like in the olden days. Avinash recollects and mentions to Kasturi many landmarks and how it was back then. She is not sure if she remembers and can correlate but what engages her is Avinash's excitement in recollecting all these. Walking down the lanes they never notice when they were hand in hand and an auto rickshaw coming straight towards them is not enough for Avinash to leave her hand. He pulls her towards him taking care of her as always and their hands stays together till they run to board the metro.

It is dark by the time they get down the train which has crossed 5 stations and 15mins. Getting down the bridge Avinash jumps one stair in between and insists that Kasturi too follows the same and she does without caring for anyone to notice them. Few heads turn towards them though. From the station to the hotel they don't even talk about auto rickshaws or cabs. Avinash tells her "come I will take you from a shortcut to our hotel." They walk through the small lanes of the market place. Avinash stops in front of a small shop and looks at Kasturi "remember, we took hair oil as you forgot to bring" and pulls her further holding her hand crossing 12-15 more shops and taking a left. He stands in front of this theatre holding Kasturi's hand tightly and says "This is where we saw the first movie together." His eyes spark as he mentions many more memories till they reach the Hotel. From the restaurant, they had food to the Hotel they boarded 23 years back during their honeymoon. Kasturi is all in tears. Words refuse to come out as they are sure they would fall short to express her emotions. Avinash is exactly aware of what she feels at that very moment and he too needs no words to be heard from her; it is all said in her look.

Avinash orders a light dinner while Kasturi calls back home to speak with Akshay and Varun. Kasturi's father conveys that they are already asleep. Kasturi sits beside Avinash on the bed placing her hand over his. Fingers cross each other merging to be one and finding the missing beat of both the hearts lost in a materialistic world.

Avinash looks into her eyes and softly says "you always said, just love me and everything else will fall in place. Now, you forgot your words." How could Kasturi accept that she forgot? She never forgot. The rest of the night passes blaming each other but with lots of laughs and loves.

The Treacherous

It is not only Rakesh's territory that shows a lack of orders but another territory that also had a good base started showing different colour.

Rakesh is senior and most trustworthy. Mohan, their Engineer at Nashik is Avinash's first Cousin. He is a simple down to earth person. The whole of their team is closely knit. Kasturi and Avinash were never like bosses to them and that was what all their employees felt good about.

The receptionist transfers a call to Kasturi while she is having her lunch, she explains that there is a call from some doctor from Sangli and he is very furious. Kasturi allows her to connect.

"Yes sir, good afternoon" she greets. The doctor is not willing to greet and directly comes to the point "Madam, your person took thirty-five thousand rupees from us and it is been 3months still our machine is not fixed." Kasturi enquires about the name of the hospital and other machine details and politely replies "sorry, sir probably you are mistaken, we have not supplied this machine to you." Further discussion reveals that the doctor is talking about Kasturi's company and he mentions Mohan's name and date when he collected cash from them. Kasturi is left with no option but to mention to him that she will look into it and call back. Kasturi conveys this to

Avinash, who takes it lightly at least for now.

Rakesh too is struggling with his orders. It is becoming very frequent that Kasturi visits Kolhapur, finalises deals, and with a heavy heart Rakesh would convey that it is gone to someone else. Kasturi and Avinash are aware that the market is changing; there are lots of freelancers in the market who are responsible for this change.

Once during Kasturi's visit and waiting for Manav's call they were just passing time sitting in the garden. She was keen to know why orders were getting diverted. Rakesh mentions that it was some new company who did not import machines but just source them locally and deliver them. Hence there is a big price difference that pushes customers towards them, Kasturi is not satisfied with this answer as she knew all the customers personally and met them during each of her visits.

Kasturi tries to further understand what exactly is going on; she asks Rakesh "Spares consumption has also gone high and mostly it is for warranty machines, this was not the case ever. Annual Maintenance contracts are also not coming; it is becoming difficult to pay your salaries and your allowances." Rakesh is not in a position to give any valid explanation. Complaints from under warranty machines slowly ruin their relationship with many customers and few among them are even those who started their career with their first machine from Kasturi's company. Though payment terms are to be against delivery of machines, it would never be so. Payments would come only in 30-90days. All complaints from under warranty machines start marking losses for the company as payments delay further due to frequent breakdowns. Avinash's visits to Kolhapur became frequent. Avinash attends many machines personally still, within 2-3 days machine status remains the same. They analyse it to be some foul play by some competitors who would tie up with the technicians and spoil their image in the market. In all these years this was the worst stage for their business.

Kasturi talks to Rakesh daily to have a close look at the market there and he too keeps on posting details. Each time they spoke or Kasturi visited she would ask for the faulty spares from Rakesh so that they can be repaired and used but their schedule would be very hectic and Rakesh failed to do so. Mumbai-based engineers find it difficult to fulfil spares requirements from Rakesh and Mohan.

One fine day Kasturi notices that Avinash is trying to avoid Mohan's call. She checks with her engineer and she is shocked. He confirms that Avinash is not on talking terms with Mohan. She could not immediately figure out and hence checked with her in-laws if there is an issue on the family front but there were none. It is only on the basis of lots of insisting that Taheer, their senior engineer in Mumbai reveals that Avinash traced the case of Mohan collecting Rs.35,000/- and found that not only this matter over many months he has been working privately and utilising spares from the company. He would ask for spares for under warranty machines and use them for fulfilling his requirement.

Mohan's territory shows an all-time low in service revenue as well. Most of the doctors who had all their machines were no longer willing to take the Annual Maintenance Contract. On enquiring with a couple of users Kasturi figures out that they were not satisfied with the response time and even if machines were attended to and fixed it would repeatedly give the same problems. Kasturi is not able to understand when spares are immediately despatched to Mohan why this issue was not sorted. Moreover, his territory was such that he should be in a position to attend calls the same day or the first half of the next day.

Things start getting worse when Mohan would convey that the machines are being attended to and customers complained that he is not attending.

Kasturi receives a call from Dr.Wagh, one of the doctors who too started his career with the first machines from her. She is expecting his call because she had submitted a quote for machines recently on his request. Kasturi picks up his call and very pleasantly greets him "good afternoon sir, how are you?"

"Yes, I am good. I saw your quote but it is too high" he mentions. They have a brief talk about the price and the current market scenario and competitor's strategies. Dr.Wagh tells her "Your engineer has quoted much less than your offer. How come? Mohan is your person right? Just an hour back he visited with the offer." Kasturi is shocked as that is not Mohan's territory and just in the morning they had a talk and he mentioned that he is in Baramati attending a call. It is not possible to complete the call and be here at Dr.Wagh's place. Dr.Wagh also reveals how and why a doctor from Malegaon is supporting Mohan and this was the same doctor for whom they had gone out of the way to help him out in his initial days. All the complaints of many customers suddenly made sense to her, where she had believed him over the customers. Overconsumption of spares, lack of orders, and delay in payments everything is clear. Avinash too confirms that he traced Mohan's activities and found him guilty beyond imagination. It is not only that he borrowed salary from them and worked privately but what harmed more is that he also utilised all company's spares and spares from under warranty machines and kept them non-functional for the wants of spares conveying to customers that despite several follow ups company is not sending spares.

This is beyond imagination for Kasturi and Avinash that he would go to such an extent. Unfortunately, by the time all these came to light, much damage was already done.

Kasturi starts sensing indifferent behaviour from Rakesh too. He is a much more mature and understanding person than Mohan. He witness how Kasturi was trying hard to get the company back on track and she appreciated the way Rakesh stood by them. After learning about Mohan's activities, Rakesh not handing over faulty spares puts him under suspicion.

By this time Manav had already left the trust. Dr.Inamdar though working in close association with the ministers and holding a big position in the trust is a very down-to-earth person. He would extend help to whoever approached him. His office is open to everyone. Patients dropped in at any point in time and he would prescribe free treatments and operations etc. for them via trust funds.

Kasturi makes a casual visit to Dr.Inamdar for a warranty that is expired for the machines supplied via trusts. Dr.Inamdaar greets her pleasantly as always. She waits sitting in his cabin while he attends to patients. Rakesh calls to convey that he is waiting downstairs to pick up Kasturi. She hangs up saying yes, coming down in 10 mins. Dr.Inamdaar looks at Kasturi with a smile asking "Rakesh?" She replies "yes sir, we have a meeting so he is down to pick me up." He smiles again "call him upstairs "she calls him, initially he is not willing to come up as they are getting late for the scheduled meeting but eventually comes. Just peeping in Dr.Inamdars cabin he wishes "good afternoon sir." Dr.Inamdaar responds "yes Rakesh, come in. Did you fix up the machine which was down? You didn't inform me." Rakesh conveys that the machine has been attended to and the report submitted. Kasturi is looking at both of them. Rakesh waits outside the cabin in the waiting area.

Dr.Inamdaar looks at Kasturi asking "How is this

person Rakesh? Is he trustworthy? Kasturi instantly replies "yes sir, he has been working with us for the past 9years and is very sincere in his work." Dr.Inamdaar while scribbling on a prescription pad looking at the patient standing in front of him utters "Sincere and trustworthy are two different things Kasturi." The patient leaves and while the other patient is about to enter Dr.Inamdar stops him saying "please come after 5mins." Patient steps back. Dr. Inamdar continues "He came to submit this report to my office and conveyed to my staff that he can supply machines at a lesser rate than the company and that he can also take machines in service contract at lesser cost." Dr.Inamdaar notices a drop in Kasturi's expressions "oh, he would be the last person I can expect this from. Had it not been coming from you sir, I would never trust this." Dr.Inamdaar further mentions "I can call him here now and whatever I would do to him, he will not only leave this field but also this place forever. We know how to show these types of persons their place. Should I call him?" Kasturi is surprised by his statement for she has never witnessed such harsh words from him ever.

Kasturi is not able to understand what was happening, while Dr.Inamdaar continued with his options to deal with and punish Rakesh. Katuri feels like a failure. Mohan, a close relative, and now Rakesh whom she trusted more than anyone else.

It didn't take long for them to discover that Mohan and Rakesh had joined hands and they were operating in this manner for more than two years. Rakesh had witnessed all that Kasturi suffered following their orders and with Manav and she always thought Rakesh was her moral support. But the fact was Rakesh was more deceptive than Manav.Kasturi could not believe how someone can behave so fake.

Right from Rakesh's first day, to his placement at Nasik then to Kolhapur, to so many visits together, to his marriage, to sponsoring his Honeymoon, to the birth of his daughter everything ran through. Kasturi recollects when she visited Rakesh's house to see his baby for the first time.

Holding the tiny little girl she kissed her forehead and Rakesh's mother's eyes are full of tears. She couldn't control her sentiments and expressed "Madam, whatever Rakesh is today is only because of you and Avinash Sir. You gave him a job and taught him work when we were in great need. My family cannot thank you enough for this." Holding the baby in one hand very carefully, Kasturi consoled Rakesh's Mom, hugging her, not saying much "Every time I have to tell this, please don't address me as Madam" and they both laugh.

All those episodes just seemed to be yesterday and today Kasturi was in tears thinking that this would have been the last thing to happen.

It was exactly two years back. Kasturi and Rakesh finished their work at Akola. The day was busy as usual and went on without lunch. It was almost 5 pm when they managed to grab some snacks at the hospital canteen. Kasturi's train is at 10.30 pm and she decides to wait in the Railway lounge till then. Rakesh had to go in the opposite direction for further calls and his train was in another half an hour. Accompanying Kasturi till then, chatting all about business, it suddenly clicks to Kasturi that she can visit Shegaon's Gajanan Maharaj Temple and take her train from Shegaon itself. She always preferred such options over sitting in the waiting room. But, travelling from Akola to Shegaon would be either in the unreserved general compartment or travel in the reserved compartment illegally.

Rakesh too opts to join her as it is too late for her to go alone and he too didn't visit the temple for years. Rakesh insists on taking a reserved compartment trying to justify saying its just one station but had to board the general compartment as Kasturi doesn't agree with his suggestion.

The compartment looked overcrowded with passengers occupying places even between sets. The crowd is mainly the labour class who would travel to the city from distant villages for their daily wages. With difficulty, Kasturi manages place for herself while Rakesh makes an unsuccessful attempt to find a seat.

Kasturi notice one middle-aged person sitting in the crowd who occupied a gap between two berths. Looking at the thick bundle of gauze tightly fastened by a broad adjustable strip on his right hand she understands that he is a Heamodiaysis patient returning after the treatment. She looks at Rakesh and points at that man with her expression. Rakesh too points out at another man with a similar bandage, hardly sitting on the edge of the upper berth. Both of them are sad to see this. In no time they notice at least 5-6 such patients travelling in that one compartment. Kasturi is not able to resist and initiates a talk with one of them. She enquires "Are you on Haemodialysis? Where are you from?" The man is more than willing to open up as if he just wanted to take out everything which was lying deep down in his heart. "What should I tell madam? For 4 years I have been travelling from my village to Akola two times a week. There is nobody to accompany me so my daughter comes along and each time she misses her classes."

Being working in this field, Kasturi is aware of the pain, and physical and psychological trauma a Kidney failure patient goes through. Rather the entire family goes through. They need to get this procedure done two or three times a week. Especially travelling from a remote village is so troublesome and when the patient is the bread earner of the family it takes a toll on the entire family.

Kasturi's eyes are filled but more than that her heart wrench with the feeling of being helpless. Not being able to do anything about this is bothering her too much.

It was then she decides to work on possibilities to make the facility available to the rural, underprivileged patients as close as possible to them.

Kasturi had many memories wherein Rakesh played an important role and now with all these difficulties Rakesh's reality shakes her from within.

Mental Convictions

Raj is not only upset with Shivsagar but feels guilty too for all that happened. He suggests Kasturi to give her and Avinash's birth dates. He mentions that he had a rough phase due to Saturn's transit and that how Murli, an Astrologer who also happens to be his close friend helped and guided him to overcome hurdles due to this phase based on his horoscope. Raj himself suggests that Kasturi also may be going through any such patch resulting in downfall.

Finding no way out, Kasturi shares the details with Raj. Another 8days time and Raj shares four audio clips which he receives from Murli. Kasturi is eager to listen to the clips but had to wait till the end of the day. She knew Avinash will not only discard any such thoughts but may even get wild on her for following all such beliefs.

Kasturi is a sincere theist while Avinash is an atheist but its ok for Avinash if Kasturi's God exists. He has always been supportive towards all rituals followed by Kasturi and would be by her side. Apart from this all these beliefs are not Avinash's cup of tea and hence it is mutually agreed between her and Raj that they would not disclose it to Avinash.

Late at night after checking that Avinash and Kids are fast asleep Kasturi silently gets up, opens the drawer of the side table, and picks a pair of airdopes. Slowly comes back and lies down in her place. Her eyes are closed as she listens to the audio clips one after another. Repeat the clips several times till she falls asleep.

Murli mentions all the good foreseen in near future. It seems too good to be true. He also mentions that she was going through Saturn's transit effect (Sade Sati) and that their efforts will now ripe sweet fruits of her good deeds. These clips give a momentary good feeling and the next morning is ready with the on-going struggle.

This triggers sense of being under the ill effects and that this is the reason for things not working out despite all efforts. Kasturi fall prey to one and all options shown on YouTube to get rid of this ill effect. This also leads to performing many rituals like burning yellow candles, burning bay leaves, lots of Rajfestation videos, etc. attract her and she lands up doing one or the other every single day. It may work, it may not but if nothing is working out then there must be some unseen, unknown reason she thinks.

This even further leads to more complications when someone figures out that many such problems started as they shifted to this bungalow. It gets so bad that she starts spending more time looking for remedies to resolve her problems. Trusts and donors for her project are now searched in the rituals and remedies.

Every day she sits reciting Gayatri Mantra and lands up talking to her house. She would address her house "I never searched for such a big house, I got directed here in such a way that it looked like you were made for us. Everyone blames that you are not good for us, prove it wrong to all. Find a way out for me, help and assist me to come out of the financial crisis."

Kasturi is in a very difficult state of mind and she is not to be blamed for that. When no door opens, the mind takes the opportunity to dig for the light from somewhere and that is what was exactly happening to her. Not realising that somewhere that small piece of pie remaining too was slipping slowly.

Her day would begin with getting scared if she missed waking up at Brahma Muhurta (a holy hour before dawn). Once out of bed, she would take a few moments to decide if she should do chanting after a bath or directly start chanting else the auspicious time would pass. Followed by routine work but chanting became mandatory before every email, every call she would make for her project follow-ups. If by any chance she misses the chants she would feel restless and anxious with the thought that nothing will work out as she missed the chants.

Kasturi is still not able to find peace in all this; rather it makes her mind and thoughts more fragile. Her mental health gets more delicate. Sleeping disorder knocks and anxiety touches a peak.

Kasturi is still determined to take her project on board and doesn't want to leave a single stone unturned. She is a strong believer in "where there is a will there is a way." Her will is strong but the way is not known hence she attempts whatever possibility comes to her mind.

Many a time like everyone Kasturi too witnessed the news of Start-ups funded by Mr.Ratan Tata. She would regularly surf for such news and not only felt motivated but this would also help that hope stay alive inside her sometimes.

This morning she is determined to write to Tata Trust about her project. But how to approach and whom exactly to approach is a big question. There arre many amongst the 'Good Morning friends' who could at least give that one contact detail but she decides to do it herself. Google is flooded with replies to "How to contact Mr.Ratan Tata." Kasturi opts for one she thinks to be genuine. With a detailed description she attached her project Report and sent a mail to the Trust on its email id she fetched from the Internet. She is aware that even expecting a response from them is asking for 'The Moon'.

With a hope that someday her prayer will be answered, she would daily open her email and check. Each day her heart would sink before she clicked inbox. Initially daily then the alternate day and then once in a while, she would check her email.

Getting desperate her mental health too starts deteriorating. Her daily Chants and Prayers are no longer peaceful. She lands up only asking for her wish to be filled. This is the time when the situation demands selling off their bungalow and again starting from scratch, Avinash already suggests so. She too is aware that probably this is the only way out but is not able to accept. All these struggles and then Kasturi's 'hopeful' stand is not easily digestible for Avinash.

The situation goes out of hand with the outbreak of Pandemic worldwide. Their operations get restricted.

She is probably aiming an arrow in the dark. The situation is too bad and unfavourable for her lookout she knew, but selling off the bungalow in this Pandemic is getting an all-time low rate which would even result in further loss. Moreover, she always has a stand that whatever happened with Femys Creations and its consequences was her responsibility. Hence, has a strong urge to find a way herself.

Kasturi keeps on searching for more options and more email ids. Google displayed the mail id and she shot up emails to all, she even lost the count.

Days would pass in the search of prospective mail ids and night would pass in search of herself. She had practically lost herself somewhere. Her writing is paused, and her singing is paused. What would be heard are only chants of Mantras! She is so hooked up with youtube that her eyes always look swollen.

From Gayatri Mantra to Narayani Stuti to Shree Suktam she lands up in just repeating and repeating. While she closed her eyes trying to sleep her mind played these chants non-stop for her.

Getting scared by her nightmares, she does not want to sleep today at all. Just sitting gives her a very bad backache but she is scared to sleep. Feeling hopeless for herself she rests her head on the pillow.

It is dark when she is walking through the Jungle with her sister and her mother taking care of each other. They stop and it is a railway station. The train is all open at the top. Big railings run through the length of the train. Three of them rush as the train halts. They get in, the train moves and passes but Kasturi finds herself still standing on the platform looking at the train and her mother and sister till the train disappears. It is darker than the dark; she takes a few steps behind, turns around and runs in search of light. Lands up in front of the mountain, it is so huge that it appears as if it will just swallow her any moment. She again runs looking behind at the mountain; the whole of the mountain is now full of waterfalls. There is a lot of water everywhere.She feels it will submerge everything.

Kasturi jumps to rescue herself and suddenly gets up gasping. Looks around and finds Avinash sleeping beside her. Her heartbeat is still high and her mind starts playing Hanuman Chalisa non-stop. She tries hard but is not able to stop herself. Kasturi gets up and stands directly under the shower without even switching ON the geyser. Comes out and looks for her phone. It is 4.15 am and it clicks to her that it is just an hour of Brahma Muhurta.

She has been reading about the benefits of getting up and Meditating at this holy hour and she feels good that she can catch up with this hour today. Trying to sit calm is next to impossible. Closed eyes trigger chants again, this continues for days.

Closing her laptop at around 11 pm after sending a

couple of emails she decides to just listen to her own recorded songs and falls asleep soon for a change. Kasturi wakes up and it is 5am, takes her airdopes out of her ears which are still hooked there throughout the night. By now it is a morning ritual for her to open her laptop before her eyes open just to check if there is any positive response from anyone to her proposal. Her eyes are heavy and she finds them difficult to open. She presses the power button and quickly splashes cold water on her eyes enabling them to open by the time her laptop starts. To her surprise, there is a reply to one of her mails. It is just a single line "my office will look into it and revert through the day." This sentence is sufficient to fuel energy in her. But her enthusiasm vanishes when there is no further response to this in the following days. Another response from a renowned trust office stating all their funds are going for Pandemic relief makes her understand that one and all trusts would divert their funds to the same cause for now.

Her project for underprivileged patients turns out to be her own need for her survival through these years. This gives her not-so-good feeling but she knows her intentions if not anyone else and what she was to get out of it was a working opportunity.

To her surprise, she receives a response from one more Trust as well and she is not disappointed for their reason too in sync with the Pandemic situation. She feels like stating to someone, "If one kid is sick we cannot ignore and keep the other one starving." But who was there to hear her? No one indeed!!

Just another LAP

Watching the television serial on Saibaba is like a daily ritual for Kasturi. She is broken from inside as she had received just NO from one and all she approached.

It is raining heavily outside and Kasturi is not able to concentrate on anything this evening. She notices that it is time for the serial. She puts the television ON. This 20-22 mins daily she gets motivated by watching small episodes the way it is depicted. Today is the story of a young boy who is having a fight over his business proposal with his father. His father is not willing to give any amount to him for his business as he feels it is below dignity for him if his son does such a small business. The son is about to leave the house. His mother stops him and offers some money for his business saying it is from her saving from daily expenses. Son refuses to take it saying that though you saved, it is father's money and I will not take it.

At that very point in time Sai Baba visits them and the boy's mother explains the situation to him seeking his advice. Sai Baba looks at both of them with a very pleasant smile and then looking at the mother mentions "You should be proud of your son and value his self-respect. He will eventually grow and succeed in his business and his life as well. You only need to direct him and help in any possible way." "But Baba, he is not taking this money from me and wants to leave this house" mother expresses her worry.

 Sai Baba explains "you have something in your house which doesn't belong to his father but it belongs to your son. Look for it and that will help." Sai Baba leaves and so does her son. The whole of the day the lady thinks and searches her belongings for that one thing that belongs to her son. She is not able to understand or recollect what that one thing is that Sai Baba is pointing at. Not getting any clue she lies down on her bed carrying a sad feeling. She doesn't give up though for the very simple reason that she has so much trust in Sai Baba that she knows if he has mentioned so, there is something which I am missing on. She keeps on thinking and recollecting. Suddenly, she notices a golden glow coming out of her cupboard. She gets up in anxiety and instantly opens the door and the glow gets intense, she opens the locker and the glow gets more intense and it is coming out of one cloth pouch. She immediately picks it up and holds it close to her heart. Glow disappears as she understands what Sai Baba was pointing at. She opens the pouch and takes out a golden bracelet from it. Her tears flow with the thought that how Sai Baba helped her find this one thing that she can offer to her son and which belongs to him.

This bracelet her father made for his grandson on his 5th birthday and now it doesn't fit him anymore so it was lying in the locker. As it is not from his father's money the boy too is convinced, takes it and starts his business.

At the end of the episode Sai Baba explains, "every person has something which belongs to them the only point is to find that out. If there is a will to do something there is a way you can achieve it, challenge is just to find that out."

Kasturi gets engrossed in this episode. When it ends she slowly gets up from the couch and walks toward the balcony. Standing there, looking at the road and the vehicles outside her thoughts wonder, do even I have something which belongs only to me and which can help me. She is fed up approaching financiers and trusts and this feeling that she too may have something which will help her at this time of despair but she fails to understand what that could be. In-line with the episode, she thinks of her ornaments but they won't be much of what she is looking for "What then?"

This episode roots in her heart and mind. Days pass and her struggle continue.

This is a lazy sunday and Kasturi does not want to do anything today. Post lunch, she gets busy organising her table and drawers. One paper gets in her hand. She looks and smiles and finds more such papers in different drawers. She gathers them and walks towards the other room. She takes out one file and places these papers too in that. Winds up her cleaning session and goes to Kitchen to prepare dinner.

Suddenly, she runs back to reach that file and takes it

out. File contains papers in big and small sizes, some lined, and some blank, some writing pads, and she start looking at each paper with passion. Gathers them all and takes them close to her heart. Her tears flow. She too has found her assets which belong to herself.

She keeps that file in her office bag with the plan to just go through it to begin with. Next 2-3days she reads and recollects how and when she has scribbled all this with absolutely no intention and also started writing sometimes back even intentionally but later they were just there in the file.

While on many of her tours and waiting times she had scribbled her experiences on whichever paper of writing pads she had then. Some were just not readable and some were not understandable. But, she has written a lot. While surfing the pages all of these episodes stand in front of her which she had never remembered but probably never forgotten too. It was already there deep down in the layers of her memories. It was just that all new and further experiences got deposited on this and now they just peep out of the layers and look at Kasturi like a small baby who looks at its mom with an innocent face saying "Mom, you just forgot me while being busy in your work." The feel of those papers in her hands is so, like holding the baby after returning home after a busy day. She feels sentimental.

Not knowing how to proceed and what to do about it Kasturi checks out with a few typists who would type it for her and then she can decide further once she has a soft copy. With a bit of exercise, she manages to give it to a lady close to her residence. Kasturi doesn't like her due to her dull and too much of let go attitude during their conversations but with not much choice Kasturi decides to go with her. She thinks it is just a typing job so not to worry.

She is supposed to return the draft in 8days and Kasturi Keeps on calling as it is been more than 20days now. Kasturi is losing patience now. Just when she thinks to go and blast her, Kasturi receives a call from her saying it is done and that the pen drive can be collected. All Kasturi's anger vanishes on hearing this. While back home from the office she collects the pen drive.

Kasturi is excited to see those words on her laptop screen. It takes a week or so to rectify typo errors. After a bit more of homework, Kasturi is finally ready with her first draft.

Looking for the options for publishing this, Kasturi comes across self-publishing platforms. She writes to 4 Publishers. She is bothered about the cost involved and with the current financial crisis; any amount is difficult to manage.

Avinash has seen her writing and has always encouraged her writing and singing as well. Though Avinash is not aware of how Kasturi is looking at her book and probably it is difficult to make him or anyone understand this but Avinash convinces her that it is alright to spend some amount for publishing, just that she should not get discouraged and give up if it doesn't earn as she feel it would.

Kasturi is not happy about the thought that she is looking upon her book as an earning source. For now, she still has lots of questions coming to her mind "will it work? Will the readers like it? Will anyone even notice and purchase her book? In the first place, is this the way a book is written?" Kasturi is in the phase where she is not confident but has to build hope at the same time. She is not a regular reader as well. All these years she had only read either Physics or Engineering books. But yes, she remembers reading just one "Like the Flowing River" by Paulo Coelho and of course how can she forget "Power of the Subconscious Mind" which Vikram gifted Avinash.

With all her not so much experience of reading, she has written these many pages and when she reads them, she feels good about it. With that small positive attitude, she finalises with one publishing house.

All the formalities of payments, signing of the contract, etc. are done. She receives a photo of options of her possible book cover; she is super excited to see the same. Her excitement fades in a couple of days as none of the options they suggest touches her heart. The cover designer shares a link and Kasturi surfs on the site. She notices that this was a free site wherein one can just log in and choose without any payments. Kasturi herself chooses one cover that she feels appropriate. She looks into her offer and the amount they had charged for cover design. Looking at the word 'Design' and all that Kasturi is asked to describe how she wants the cover to be and she is under the impression that there will be a designer who would customise her book cover but it is just about picking up one photo from all those options available for free.

The process starts and she receives a call from the editing team. The lady editor is so sweet to talk with a thin and crisp voice she conveys "Madam, I have gone through your book and your writing is excellent" Kasturi feels overwhelmed. The lady continues "But, it needs thorough editing. There are so many grammatical mistakes and this draft needs more corrections. Kasturi is in agreement with the lady and conveys, "Yes I know. The way it is written and the typist being non-English typist. I am aware it needs editing. Hence I selected the package with editing. If you want I shall share the package details."

"You are right madam but that's only basic editing. If you go for thorough editing it will cost you more over your current package" she clarifies.

Kasturi is again disturbed, she is under the impression that once said amount is paid and editing is included no other expense is further involved but she is wrong. Kasturi faces a challenge in dedicating time to her book now. Her business and her kids are overpowering her will to publish her book. Moreover, she gets motion sickness if she reads while trying to edit the draft while she travels.

The editing part makes her feel a little more than cheated, all the passes she goes through post their so-called editing her grammatical mistakes are hardly covered. Finally, leaving the thought behind that 'I have paid for this and they need to do it', Kasturi takes two days off and tries it herself. With so much in her mind and all that entangled emotions she just wraps it up. It seems ok to her now though.

Publishers release the promotional video and all her anger toward them diminishes. It has come up so well. Mention of Context as written by her close friend appears through the video and reading those lines Kasturi gets goosebumps. It may not be a great thing for the rest of the world but it is her creation, shaping up in front of her.

Website and Facebook page mentioning her as 'AUTHOR' adds to her excitement all the more. She shares the video clip with all her friends and family and all of them are surprised to see her new facet. All their calls and messages are overwhelming.

She sends her final approved draft to the publishers and according to them; it is just another week now. She waits desperately to announce her book.

Act of Understudy

While working for companies Kasturi always attended service calls even when her boss insisted on shifting her to sales. She was an engineer and she loved to have hands-on machines. The satisfaction of repairing and setting the machine right was incomparable. She felt a big achievement for completing even the smallest call.

As an entrepreneur it is different. It is starting from scratch, growing your business, and being your own office boy, your own typist, your own receptionist, all in one to begin with. You cannot deny sales calls, you cannot insist only on your satisfaction from service calls.

Kasturi gets moulded as an entrepreneur. Steady business and addressing her passion for travelling, meeting people, cracking deals, and so on. Where good business relationships were blooming some customers would default on payments and try to take advantage.

One busy morning she hears the beep of her cell phone and not paying much attention to it she carries out her cooking. Later in the afternoon, she is just scrolling through the messages and she notices this message which beeped in the morning. It said your case no 12/2019 is due for hearing on 23rd January 2019. She couldn't get what was that about, she just screamed and called Avinash. He was working on a machine and didn't pay much attention to her. She gets up from her chair and rushes toward him. She utters that message on her cell phone "see, this message; what case?" Avinash takes her mobile and reads the message completely which mentions 'at Warud consumer court'. Both of them take no time to understand the context of the message.

This doctor from Warud, not personally known to them but had placed an order for the machine. He approaches them through some known doctor and insists on quick delivery for his hospital inauguration is scheduled shortly and Kasturi insists on 100% advance but negotiations land upon 50% advance and 50% against installations. Equipment is supplied and the doctor fails to give a balance of 50% at installation.

Kasturi has tough time following up with him for balance payments. Each time he complains about the machine's performance and makes excuses while the engineer attends the calls and finds the machine to be working.

Days pass and one fine day doctor calls her asking to replace the existing machine with the upgraded version giving an excuse that this is not performing up to their satisfaction. Kasturi puts it up to him that the machine can be replaced by an upgraded version but he will need to pay the difference amount and only then it can be done. Listening to this the doctor gets wild and says "since installation it is not performing and I have lost business due to this and so you should give me an upgraded version at the same cost. Kasturi tries to make her point clear by putting it to him that it is not possible as the difference is not a small amount. He threatens to approach consumer court if she

She is more than wild on him. Avinash tries to calm
her down saying, "let me go and check on the
specified day then we will see how to go about it."
Kasturi is not in agreement and she herself wants to
go as this was her deal. Avinash knew that there was
no point in arguing and gently tap her back saying "let
us take some time and decide, don't panic." Kasturi
gives a look to Avinash expressing that it is not a
panic, its anger!

Avinash visits consumer court on the specified date
just to know that only the lawyer needs to file the
documents that day and then take a further date.
Avinash is not prepared for this and requests a further
date. He speaks to a couple of lawyers about their fees
and all and also takes their contact numbers.

On the next date, Kasturi gets down from the
crowded and dusty state transport bus at the Warud
bus depot. Asks one autorickshaw fellow for the
address who offers to drop her at the court
mentioning that it is far and not within walking
distance. She gets in and looks at the city while he
drives. In another 10-12mins he halts near a huge
structure saying this is the court. Kasturi gets down
questioning, "This?" by the time one person
approaches them enquiring "what are you looking
for?" Kasturi takes no time to respond to "consumer
court." Unexpectedly she gets the answer "oh, you
have come to the wrong place; it is very close to the

bus stand." Kasturi looks at the autorickshaw guy and he immediately apologises saying "oh that one? I will drop you back, don't worry." By this time the helping guy introduces himself as a Lawyer and offers to help "follow my bike; I am going the same way." They reach the consumer court and he extends his help by guiding her to the exact place where she needs to approach. Looks into the submission papers she carries with her and guides further "you should ask for a change in Jurisdiction from Warud to Mumbai." Oh, is it possible? She is eager to know. Yes, else this doctor will make you run from Mumbai to here. Kasturi mentions to him that it is normally written in the terms and conditions of the offer and also Invoice "subject to Mumbai Jurisdiction." Listening to this he insists on preparing a fresh submission for a change of Jurisdiction. After consulting Avinash she agrees to prepare a fresh submission as the lawyer guides. He also directs her further for where it is to be submitted and leaves without charging anything for this guidance but doesn't forget to leave his number for further correspondence.

The court is yet to open; Kasturi is more than hungry by now. She walks out of the premises and finds a small stall just across the road. Hesitantly she peeps in and an old man invites her "Please come we serve hot samosas and creamy lassi. Kasturi couldn't resist and slowly enter. Sitting on a bench in front of the table gives her a school-ly feeling. The place is small with a typical village ambiance. The aroma of smoky coal and frying samosas is like heaven for her. She doesn't take much time to grab that satisfying mouthful bite and the sip of lassi. She praises the serving too much and offers the old man some more amount than the bills. He refuses saying customer satisfaction is more than anything in the world. He extends the discussion by saying "I have a big land and both my sons are grown up and married, well settled with their jobs. I run this small restaurant just to kill my time." She is happy to chat with this person for some more time before leaving.

Entering the courtroom she notices one person sitting in one corner and she has no option but to enquire with him. She approaches him "Sir, my case is listed for today, where should I submit these papers? He asks for the paper saying "what is it?" and Kasturi hands over the paper to him. He looks at them and says, "Why are you requesting a change of Jurisdiction? You will be heard here genuinely." He guides her for something missing in the submission and writes that on her do   `cuments just to help her out. He understands that these legalities are not her cup of tea and checks if she has appointed any lawyer. She nods expressing 'no'.

He tells her to sit and calls the office boy to offer her water when she mentioned that she is coming from Mumbai. He leaves before the office boy gets her a glass of water. Handing over a glass of water to her, office boy mentions "Saheb (*Sir*), helped you to complete your papers!!" She is surprised "who Saheb?"He tells her that the person who helped her with writing some details is the Senior Judge here. "Oh, I didn't know. But he is a nice person. Office boy continues, "Saheb doesn't talk to anyone, but he helped you, you are lucky." Kasturi passes a tiny smile while handing over the glass back.

This is the first time she is experiencing the courtroom. It is a bit different from what she has seen in the movies. She thinks maybe consumer courts are different. There are three Judges; two male and one female. She is aware that all of them noticed her since she has been waiting there since the court begins.

She waits in the courtroom while other cases are heard, in between checking with the registrar for when is her turn expected. Post Lunch before the Judges take their chair, a young lady lawyer enters and occupies a chair in the adjacent row. Casually Kasturi passes a smile to her and she doesn't respond. Judges enter the courtroom and as they occupy their seats the lady Judge looks at the female lawyer saying "You have come and not Pawar saheb? She replies promptly "He is presenting a case in district court" Judge also enquires about the wellbeing of Pawar saheb. While this conversation is going on this lady lawyer passes a look at Kasturi which she fails to understand what the expressions mean when she doesn't even know who the female is that she was a junior Lawyer to the senior lawyer of the district whom this doctor hired for her case.

Judges asks for the submission of papers and enquires with Kasturi if her lawyer is also present; she explains that this is the first time she is visiting and that she is yet to appoint one. Something clicks in her mind and she casually asks "Can, I present my case myself, sir? " Yes of course, by all means," the Judge replies. "And what if I want to appoint one in between?" Judge clarifies, "You can present your case and at any point of time if you feel then you can complete the formalities and appoint a lawyer." Kasturi is happy to hear that. She Hands over the paper to the Registrar and eventually Registrar to the Judge. Judge indirectly tries to convince her "You have asked for a change of Jurisdiction but don't worry we will hear you fairly and there won't be any injustice to you. She responds" I understand sir and have full faith in this honourable court but it is not easy to follow up from Mumbai."

She feels that the approach of a lawyer may or may not be right. Possibility of only extending further dates and risk of joining hands with the opposition party prevails.

The judge accepts Kasturi's submission and gives her the next date. As she comes out of the courtroom a female lawyer follows her offering her to drop upto the bus stand. Kasturi is hesitant but eventually agrees. Down from her bike near the bus stand the lady lawyer doesn't forget to mention "If you are interested in a settlement just let me know, I shall try to convince my client "Kasturi's eyebrows are raised in surprise as she notices the reason behind the helping gesture and instantly replies "we are not at fault and doctors should understand that they cannot take advantage of being in a noble profession. See you" she completes.

Kasturi grabs all the thoughts on whether taking up the case and presenting herself is the right decision or not. She calls her father who is a lawyer and he seconds her decision without a second thought. She is aware that it is not going to be easy as she will have to be present for every date and do a lot of study about the law concerning the consumer act.

Back home, Avinash tries to convince her to hire a lawyer so that she need not go for each date, and lots of time when it is only about allocating the next date, her visit will be just a waste. Discussing the pros and cons of all this they mutually agree to Kasturi presenting the case for herself.

Her plea for a change of Jurisdiction is not accepted on the ground that they don't have any such agreement signed and only based on its mention on the Invoice is not sufficient to be considered. She is sad as it means many more visits. The opposition lawyer gives a sarcastic smile and it pokes Kasturi.

Studying the soft copy of the submission she realises that the descriptions are not as she had mentioned to the lawyer who made it for them before she left for Warud. Rectifying the same, keeping the legal format intact is not tough. She mails the final draft to her father and he is impressed with her. He praises "you should have become a lawyer "and both laugh.

Her journey continues. The next time to Warud is very peaceful as she is prepared with the draft and she knows the proceedings by now. She gets down at Amravati station. She checks-in the station restroom.

Quickly freshens up and heads towards the bus stand in an auto rickshaw. Waiting for the bus to Warud is not very pleasant and finally grabs the front seat next to the conductor as the bus emerges through the dusty cloud.

Walking from the Warud bus stand to the consumer court is another pleasant experience for her which she enjoys each time passing from there. On her left side are all small huts emitting a smoky aroma from their kitchen where food is cooked on cow-dung cake." On the right side are small stalls trying to set up for the day.

She usually reaches her destination at least two hours before the court opens and sits on the veranda built around a huge tree. In front of her are three huge trees with no leaves on them. They look huge and strong. Their strong stems are all white-skinned and give a very gigantic look. Eventually Kasturi starts taking them as companions while she waits there on all her further dates.

Getting down at Shegaon station, walking down to Gajanan Maharaj temple in the twilight at 5am, freshening up there, attending morning aarti, then having Mahaprasad before leaving for Amravati to finally reach Warud had become routine now. All that irritation for the day ahead while attending her court case is left behind and she takes it lightly with the confidence that she is right and she will win.

At the end of one such day while she returns to Amravati station after getting exhausted by waiting for her turn in court and the wrenching journey she enters the waiting room. Talking to her fellow passengers kills her waiting time as usual. There is still time for her train and she opens her mail because she has not checked it throughout the day.

Surfing the mails she notices a mail from her publisher and a link, it is the Amazon Prime Link of her book to place an order. She feels excited, quickly clicks it and it opens the order page. Seeing her book on the Amazon Platform is an out of the world feeling. She shares it on Facebook with a small write-up. She also shares with all her friends and family and instantly receives comments and words of appreciation.

While checking the replies Kasturi notices a message from Manav, she thinks she forwarded the message by mistake but she hasn't. He has sent her a screenshot of the order placed for her book. She realises probably that's the first order for her book which was just within no time the link was out. And, now she is not surprised about how he knows about it. Kasturi responds with a thumbs-up emoji.

Next few days orders keep on pouring and so do the reviews on Amazon but the intensity vanish with the passing time. With all her allotted amount going into publishing she is left out with nothing for marketing. Publishers have given her all possible tools for marketing but again promoting is another unaffordable expense for now.

One fine day she notices that after Manav's message

about the purchase of her book she has not received any message from him whatsoever, no greeting messages, nothing. Finally, for his own reasons Manav puts an end to his chapter from his side as well.

It is been a year and more since she is following up and finally, they get a date for the final hearing. She recollects all the dates when the opposition party would purposefully come very late making her sit the whole day. But all these times she heard and witnessed many cases. Had samosas and lassi many a time and chats with the tall and strong trees regularly.

This was the final day. Her heart was experiencing mixed emotions and slight worry "what if we lose?" It would be a big setback. Many people with whom she shared this had presented their opinion as the local doctor would influence the Judges but somewhere Kasturi's heart assured her that Justice prevails.

Finally a night before the final hearing she leaves her house well in time to catch the train but gets delayed due to local train delays.

She runs at maximum speed after hearing the announcement of her train. That stretch from platform No.1 to platform No.5 of Thane station is not much but to run cutting peak hour crowds is always tough. Moreover, if the destination is not where you wish to go it makes it all the farther and feet all the more heavier. She rushes to enter the compartment of the train. Gasping for breath sits on the side berth passing a tiny smile at a fellow passenger. Her phone rings, and within no time she answers "made it, I had almost missed the train today." Nodding for a couple of more seconds in response to whatever Avinash said she disconnects saying "take care."

By now she is comfortable, sipping water from the bottle as the young man sitting opposite her winds up and climbs to the side upper berth. She stretches her legs, squeezing her both arms by herself, trying to release her tiredness. Closing her eyes and resting on the edge of the side window, she falls asleep.

A sudden jerk due to the halting of the train breaks her sleep. Trying to open heavy eyelids, she focuses on the station name which reads 'Nashik'. "Three hours passed" she murmurs to herself, quickly arranges bed and lies down. The train picks up speed and so does her anxiety. She tries to adjust herself to grab her sleep back, but in vain.

Turning to face the window while lying down, she pulls the window curtain to one side and the waning moon in the clear sky is at her sight. Her lips smile and a slight gleam in her eyes remains unnoticed by the rest of the world.

This day and her very first visit, she is travelling to Warud. Sometimes In 3tier AC or sleeper class or even on RAC status, sometimes bus from Warud till Thane but never missed any date. That 2hrs journey from Amravati to Warud tried to break her at times and her decision of fighting the case herself rather than opting for a lawyer felt wrong when poky heat, rolling sweat on her temples and back irritated.

Recollecting all her visits to Warud she de-boards the train at Amravati and heads towards the bus stand. After almost 50mins the bus emerges out of a dust cloud and as usual she manages to snag a seat for herself.

The complainant's lawyer being senior and well known in the district had never bothered her. Whatever 2-3 times she faced him while arguing, she presented her case confidently. Legal guidance from her father and a lawyer friend made additions to her vocabulary with words like Adverse Inference and she understood the definition of 'Consumer' like never before.

Her study on the Consumer Protection Act, her analytical skills, responsiveness, and investigation skills all flaunted in that courtroom while she presented her counterargument on the previous date. Her lawyer friend and Avinash who attended this were well satisfied by the way she proved how a consumer takes advantage of the protection act, how the doctor's so-called evidence was inappropriate, and how he tried to exploit the company and the owners with false allegations.

She gets down at Warud bus Stand. Walking towards the court, she thinks "this might be my last visit here. If the doctor wins, we will have to go to the higher court where primarily depositing part of the doctor's claim of 18 lacs may be mandatory before a case is even admitted. If we win, we win. He may not want to waste time and money again."

Sitting and talking to her companion trees she looks at the entrance of the court and recollects her previous visit where she had to physically present her counter-argument.

The Doctor's lawyer walks into the courtroom followed by his junior lawyers. Kasturi wishes him, "Hello sir, how are you?" He just nods showcasing his seniority in this profession and occupies a seat in the front row. The Lady lawyer who normally greets Kasturi doesn't dare to even look at her in front of her boss. Kasturi doesn't mind it as she understands her position.

Registrar announces their case no. to be heard. The doctor's lawyer stands and is about to present this case himself for the first time. While Petitioner and Opponent have already given their submissions with the copy of the same to each other it is expected that they have thoroughly gone through each other's evidence which they would produce and give the counter-argument for the same.

The doctor's lawyer begins...

"My lord; my client purchased a machine from this company and it was never functional. My Client runs a reputed Hospital and due to the non-performance of the machine hospital lost a lot of patients and business and hence we claim for 18 lacs as compensation and also interest on that till the case is settled." He also submits a WhatsApp chat history between the Doctor and Kasturi trying to prove that the doctor conveyed about the faults in the machine and her engineer visited twice but couldn't fix it. He emphasises compensation and loss of reputation several times before closing his argument." He takes his seat

and there is so much silence in the room that the murmurs of his junior lawyers attract a "shh" from the registrar.

Lady Judge looks at Kasturi raising her hand to present her counter-argument. Kasturi looks at Avinash before standing in front of the forum, who is accompanying her this time. She starts by saying "good evening. I, Kasturi, am here to present a counter-argument on behalf of my company as well as both the directors of the company. Myself being one of them." She is a bit more formal compared to her opponent. Not being from the faculty she had prepared to be up to the mark.

Her counter-argument begins.

"Sir, firstly I would like to mention the definition of a CONSUMER."

The doctor's lawyer laughs, now you will teach us? Kasturi is not at all distracted by his reaction while Judge looks at him with a slight disappointment for his reflex saying "please let her speak."

Kasturi continues while handing over three copies of a few pages from the Consumer Protection Act "sir, according to the Consumer Protection act.

"Any person who obtains the goods for resale or commercial purpose is not a consumer- The term 'for resale 'implies that the goods are brought to sell them, and the expression 'for commercial purpose' is intended to cover cases other than those of resale of goods.

When goods are bought to resale or commercially exploit them, such buyer or user is not a consumer under the Act."

"I have already mentioned in my submission that the complainant is MD (Medicine) and not a Nephrologist by academics." He has purchased the machine and has to hire a Nephrologist under whose supervision Patients need to be dialyzed.

This means he is not a direct user of the machine.

She briefs further as mentioned in the act "If any person purchases a car and drives it to earn his living out of it then he/she is a consumer but, if a person purchase a car and then hire a driver and use car as earning source then the person is not falling under the category of consumer."

Repeated claim by a doctor for his loss of Rs.5000/- per day makes it obvious that the machine was intentionally purchased for commercial purposes looking at it as an additional earning source. As mentioned by respectable senior Advocate they lost money due to the non-performance of the machine and hence claims for 18 lacs for the same. Hence the complainant doctor does not fall under the category of Consumer.

Kasturi again hands over a few documents to the registrar for the Judges to refer the same mentioning " Copy of Revision Petition No.1425 of 2016 (against the order dated 15/01/2016 in Appeal No.694/2013 of the State Commission Punjab) from National consumer Dispute Redressal Commission, New Delhi is enclosed for Honourable forum's kind reference."

So, I request the honourable forum to consider this point and dismiss the case.

Secondly, according to the doctor, the machine was never

installed." She looks at the Doctor's lawyer saying "right sir?" he just raises both his eyebrows while Kasturi hands over three copies of a paper cutting to the registrar and as usual he passes them to the three of the Judges.

Kasturi explains "For your understanding sir, without going into much technical details I would like to just briefly talk about the process of Haemodialysis for which the said machine is used.

In Kidney failure patient's urea, creatinine, and other impurities which are filtered by the Kidney and drained out of the body through urine, this doesn't happen and so all these impurities accumulate in the blood. This process of filtration is carried out by an artificial kidney by using Haemodialysis machine. The machine prepares dialysate fluid with the help of water and two more concentrates. An artificial kidney is just like a box filled with straws. Imagine blood passing from inside the straws and the dialysate concentrate passing from the gap in between the straws but in the opposite direction."

Doctor's lawyer interrupts in between saying "objection, why doesn't she talk about the case only."

Kasturi looks at him and with a raised voice she says" I am exactly talking about the case sir, be little patient. She continues "Machine helps pumping out blood which passes through artificial kidney where exchange of electrolytes take place and impurities are filtered and machine pumps in the blood back to the patient body. Sir, this is a local newspaper which is exactly one month after we delivered the machine. In our absence the machine was switched ON and not only that without our certification of completing machine installation or without the electrolyte report patient was dialyzed on the machine. If you see the photograph you can see the machine connected to the patient. This is putting the patient's life at risk sir. Also importantly, paper cutting is sufficient evidence to prove that the machine delivered by us was not faulty and rather it was fully functional." Kasturi looks at the doctor's lawyer saying "to understand the seriousness of the procedure it was important to explain the same."

Kasturi continues, "Sir, I would like to brief you on a few more points...

No.1 – Complainant did not comply with his assurance of completing 50% and issuing a post-dated cheque at delivery of the machine. We repeatedly called for the machine to be commissioned. Commissioning was pending due to the unavailability of required consumables from the complainant end which are required for machine commissioning. Kasturi's voice again rises, mentioning "and that was so life-threatening for the patient. As for this case, there is no installation and the commissioning report signed hence the deal is not yet complete and hence liability doesn't come to us yet.

No.2. Complainant mentions in pt.no.10 of his rejoinder submitted that the paper cutting does not prove that the machine in the photo is one supplied by us and that he has two more Haemodialysis machines but the complainant has not submitted any proof which proves this. They had requested for early delivery of a machine for inauguration as he had no other machine at the time of inauguration which is also evident from the WhatsApp chat history submitted by them."

"No3. Sir, we have not at all received any post-dated cheques from the complainant even after repeated follow-ups. I have submitted a copy of the mail sent by the doctor dated

26.11.2018 which clearly states, "I have not paid 1lac balance payment as the machine is not working up to my satisfaction. This is another lie sir. It is one lac twenty-four thousand five hundred rupees to be precise. Hence, it proves from the documents submitted by the complainant himself that the complainant's repeated mentions that he issued post-dated cheques for balance payment is a repeated lie. Sir, the entire complaint is based on all lies without any proof." Doctor's lawyer stands up angrily objecting to her statement and she cuts him in between immediately "do you have any proof, any acknowledgment that any person from my company has received your cheques?"

Again looking at the Judges she continues "no sir, there is no such proof as they never issued cheques."

"Further sir, Rs.5000/- loss per day is claimed by the complainant. With one machine normally 2-3 Haemodialysis can be considered to be done per day. Considering the use of the machine to its maximum capacity, three Haemodialysis per day can be considered and any minimal earning unit cannot earn more than 100 Rs. per dialysis which sums up to Rs.300/- per day. Hence, for earning Rs.5000/- per day one has to perform 50 Haemodialysis per day on a single machine.

I would also like to clarify to the honourable forum that Haemodialysis running time for one session is a minimum of 4hours and there has to be at least 30mins gaps in between two consecutive Haemodialysis for disconnecting the previous patient, preparing of next patient, and connecting the next patient. Hence, logically if 50 Haemodialysis is to be carried out in 24hours then the complainant has to explain the calculation to the honourable forum for how is it possible?"

Sir, Doctor has submitted a letter mentioning his Capabilities to carry out Haemodialysis. It again comes from some private institute which is not an authorised body for the same. Moreover, it is a question that the complainant is authorised to run Haemodialysis Unit independently without a Nephrologist and not if he feels he is capable. Also, the complainant fails to submit his Medical Registration Certificate issued under the Maharashtra Medical Council Act which leads to the question of its existence and also opinion from the Medical Council of India (MCI) if a complainant is entitled to practise Nephrology based on his registration with MCI and also if he is eligible to independently run Haemodialysis unit without backup/attachment of DM or DNB Nephrologist.

Hence, we request the honourable forum to draw Adverse Inference against the complainant for not filing any say on our application dated 20/08/2019 and our response dated 25/11/2019 to the complainant's rejoinder.

The complainant also fails to submit complete WhatsApp chat history between the complainant and myself. It is clear that the complainant intentionally tries to hide the facts by producing only part of the chat."

Kasturi picks up the printout and pointing at the paper with a pen in her left-hand show it to the Judges saying "If complete chat history is produced it will reveal all the false allegations on us and also if customised phone bill was submitted by the complainant as requested by us then it will reveal that it was me who made several calls and not the complainant. Of Course, my calls were for follow-up for balance payment."

Kasturi is not willing to stop her counter argument; all her stored-up spite of the past one and half years is venting out. She repeats *"the complainant has purely used our good faith for his selfish purpose. He ordered refurbished machines for the sake of inauguration and later on for the false monetary claims. Rejoinder submitted by them is full of false allegations and false claims for monetary gains and has absolutely no proof or shreds of evidence."*

"I want to bring to the kind notice of honourable forum that all the documents starting from the complaint, written statement, rejoinder, etc. submitted by complainant only emphasise compensation which clearly shows that it is a pre-planned strategy to order the machine, use it for the inauguration and then make the monetary claim."

Kasturi closes her submission stating...

"It is, therefore, most respectfully prayed that the complaint is dismissed with the cost to the complainant and that our outstanding payment of Rs.124,800/- be recovered from the complainant along with 18% interest, in the interest of Justice as we have gone through the mental and physical harassment and any other suitable order be passed so that nobody else tries to take undue advantage of the consumer protection Act."

Kasturi rests herself on the chair, satisfied with her submission. She feels relaxed and is not bothered about anyone else's reaction to her argument and is least bothered about what the doctor's lawyer said in his closing statement before he leaves carrying his attitude and giving a not so pleasing look at Kasturi which she notices from the corner of her eye.

All of this flashback rolls in front of Kasturi today. Even on this anxious day, she is in no mood to skip her samosa, lassi and chat with the restaurant owner.

Walking towards the consumer court strong, tall, and leafless companions on the way compliment her back as she looks with admiration in her eyes for them. It is 12 noon as she reaches the court. Registrar mentions "Madam, results are normally announced 3pm onwards" She nods and occupies a chair and witnesses a couple of on-going cases as usual, probably last time now.

At around 3.15 pm registrar calls for Case no. 20/2019 and she gets up, and so does a white-haired senior lawyer accompanied by the Doctor. The Judge reads out "Case dismissed on the grounds of 'Adverse Inference'. She sighs as goose-bumps run over. She bows at the panel of judges with a smile expressing her gratitude. She notices expressions of the senior Judge and there is this unuttered conversation between Kasturi and him where he expresses that he did Justice and she thanks him from the bottom of her heart.

Outside the courtroom doctor waits with his lawyer and a taunt "madam, you won. I lost money in this case; you too lost money and time, isn't it? I made you run from Mumbai to Warud for more than a year." That sarcastic smile on his face appears prominent but is not able to overshadow her satisfaction. She looks straight into his eyes "Thanks doc for spending on my learning."

Way to the Dawn??

Kasturi is returning from her cousin's wedding. Anjali, her ex-employee, rings up. It is just a courtesy call and nothing more. She feels good to talk to Anjali. Today she had called just to convey that she had again switched her Job 6months ago and is working for this Diagnostic firm now. In 6months she made good progress and is thankful to Kasturi for advising her to switch to the Diagnostic field if she gets a good opportunity.

During her talks, Anjali mentions that they are looking for a dealer for Mumbai and Kasturi grasps this. She feels inappropriate to talk at this time but makes it a point to call her in a couple of days.

Kasturi briefs her about their current status and Anjali is shocked to know about Rakesh and Mohan but is more than happy to learn about Kasturi's interest in her company's dealership. Anjali offers to visit their house and brief them about the same. She visits and briefs all about the business, finance required, staff required, etc. It looks doable but leaves a big question mark behind.

Where will the initial investment come from?

This question haunts Kasturi for the next two days till Anjali calls again. Though in a dilemma of how she would convey it to her that the initial investment is a problem, Kasturi sounds enthusiastic as ever. "Hi Anjali, I was expecting your call." "Good morning Ma'am, I spoke to my sir and he said we can go ahead with this dealership. I will just fix up the meeting for tomorrow if you and Avinash Sir are available." Kasturi comfortably hiding her hesitation casually checks up with Anjali "Is there any possibility of a bank guarantee over cash purchase of your products for dealers?" Unexpectedly Anjali replies "of course Ma'am just that your margin will reduce a bit. Kasturi is relieved by this reply. What comes to her mind next is what would be the Bank guarantee requirement and prerequisites?

Bhushan, Anjali's immediate boss, is impressed with Kasturi and Avinash and their market Knowledge. Meeting concludes satisfactorily for both parties. This company is giant and being their dealers more opportunities would be available for them. Being Multinational there is a lot of protocol to be followed. The company will have to go through scrutiny and some certification. Kasturi tries to explore all the possibilities for arranging funds and exploring the Bank guarantee option. She understands that their house or their small piece of land at Wada may turn out to be helpful for a Bank guarantee.

Where Avinash doesn't leave any stone unturned to sell off Wada property, Kasturi follows up for a Bank guarantee with the finance company where their bungalow is mortgaged.

Almost two months passed now since the meeting

and submission of all relevant documents to Taurus but there is no response. Kasturi tries calling up Anjali but to her surprise, she doesn't respond like before. Intermittent replies to WhatsApp messages still keep hope going.

By this time Avinash almost loses hope as there is no concrete reply from Anjali and nothing is getting worked out for funds as well. It is only on receipt of a one-line mail from the company that Avinash learns and convey's to Kasturi as well that they are not being considered for the dealership due to some technical reason. As for Avinash, that's the end of this attempt but Kasturi goes by her nature and fails to give up. She calls Anjali and again there is no response from her. Kasturi drops the message but still no revert. Looking at Kasturi's hope Avinash unwillingly calls the administrator of the company just to know that the technical reason behind the rejection of the dealership is nothing but the Strike-off of their company, which they are not aware of.

A few months back, Kasturi thinks she is lucky enough to save the funds from blocking and Sudesh's suggestion of opening another bank account suffice their needs to operate but they never realised that it was not so simple and it would cost them this opportunity for the company to survive. Kasturi reminded Sudesh a couple of times about completing the formalities so that the bank account can be made active again. But, never really took it seriously as she too never knew the operations of the account being blocked, and they didn't know that the status of the company was 'Strike-off' until It came from Taurus Medicare.

The technical clearance is needed in the specified time. It is important to fix the deadline. Anjali takes a call on this and though Kasturi commits to getting everything from their end organised by Jan end, Anjali seals the date to be 31st March. Kasturi is by this time too desperate to start this venture but has no option but to go with Anjali's decision.

While Avinash is working hard to make the ends meet Kasturi gets engaged trying to find the way out. Not feeling too good today, Kasturi opts to complete paperwork from home. She feels lazy. The House matter is resolved but EMIs are a burden as the business is at an all-time low. Half of the day she spends watching a movie but her mind is occupied in search of some way out of this mess.

Post having late Lunch while continuing with the movie Kasturi recollects about making some payments. She winds up with a lazy lunch and opens her Laptop sitting on the dining table. The account had received some payments from recent sales and this small figure is rare in the account these days. Looking at the figures she sighs and before she could do the first transaction her mobile beeps and beeps again distracting her. She enters the one-time password just looking at the mobile and picks it up as she reads 'Transaction successful'. Kasturi opens the message and fails to understand what it meant because she had just completed the transaction. The message from the bank was "Your account bearing account no XXXX is freezed, please contact the branch for further details." Getting a bit anxious over this she carries out another payment and that too is done.

The message from the bank repeats a couple of more times making her more worried. She tries to reach out to her relationship manager but his number is busy. Just to checkout she again transfers some amount to her salary account and this too is done. Not able to reach the relationship Manager she decides to transfer some amount to Avinash's salary account as well and that is also done. She is not able to understand the message as transactions are still completed and then "what is this message from the bank then? "She thinks to herself. Getting a little anxious over this she calls Sudesh who picks up before a single ring is completed.

"Yes Kasturi, How are you?" he asks

"Sudesh, I am intermittently receiving this message from the bank saying "Your account bearing account no XXXX is freezed, please contact the branch for further details" but I can transfer the amount from that account. What would it be?"

Sudesh sounds worried "Oh, if you are still able to transfer, please go ahead and transfer everything to your and Avinash's account first, then we will talk."

Kasturi senses something is wrong asaa Sudesh talks. She hangs up without uttering anything and opens the account again praying that the transaction should be carried out as this was the only amount available to them. Not following Sudesh's instruction to transfer equal amounts in her and Avinash's account she transfers the majority of funds to her account leaving behind Rs.8000/-. She feels relieved to see the transaction successful. Not wanting to take a chance with the leftover amount she again initiates a transfer of Rs.5000/- to be transferred to Avinash's account and the account says 'account blocked, contact your branch'. She thanks God for not following Sudesh's instructions for this one time. She is not aware of whether that's right or wrong but that amount which they had received was the only amount available and if it was blocked they would have had a tough time. She calls back Sudesh and he too is glad that she didn't opt for two transactions. She is keen to know the reason for this. Sudesh borrows some time from her to find it out.

Kasturi makes a quick call to Avinash briefing him all about this and then again tries to connect to the bank. This time Ketan picks "Good afternoon Madam, sorry I could not take your call as I was in a meeting."

Kasturi replies "No problem. Ketan, our account is blocked. Can you guide me to why it is so?" He too is surprised and keeps Kasturi on hold to find it out from his back office. He conveys "Madam Non-compliance of filing with ROC from companies end has resulted in this." She checks up on what can be done but he just conveys that the company's Chartered Accountant will be able to guide. Kasturi calls back Sudesh and conveys this, he again asks for some more time. Kasturi finishes with the climax of her on going movie which she is watching with several pauses throughout the day before receiving a call from Sudesh.

Sudesh explains to Kasturi and she is annoyed with his team when he hears what he says "My office somehow did not file a yearly report to ROC, The Registrar of companies (ROC) and hence your account is blocked." She doesn't know all these procedures but enquires that how come without notice they do this. Sudesh explains further that this filing was not done for more than two years and probably ROC must have sent notice to their registered address.

Now, when Taurus Medicare is willing to give the dealership and all at their end is through it is a major blow if this is the reason for strike-off for not being able to work for Taurus Medicare and that too at this crucial time. This dealership can be a big breakthrough in the current scenario while struggling with the financial crisis. Their worry rises as they learn that Sudesh is Covid positive and now his subordinate Francis would be the option to get this strike-off sorted out. He is the very one responsible for the stick-off.

After months of follow-up Avinash cracks a deal in Cairo, this itself would be able to fund the complete working capital required for this dealership opportunity but it is going to take some time by the time this order is commissioned and actual profit is in hand. Avinash is set to put all his energy into this while Kasturi is left out with no option but to get this thing of strike-off sorted before Taurus Medicare gives upon them. She understands that her project of Heamodialysis units sanctioned by some trust, some Philanthropist, some donor, some Government Scheme, it is so big that it is not going to come easy way. The only practical solution in front of them currently is this dealership.

For a few days, she regularly contacts Francis and his office to know the status. It doesn't take much time for her to understand that nothing is moving from Francis's end. She gets ready and without informing Francis reaches his office. It is noon and Francis has just left for some meeting and is expected back only till 3.30 pm. His receptionist Ramola connects a call to Francis and he is on the line but Kasturi refuses to talk and conveys that she will wait and talk to Francis when he comes back to the office.

Francis enters his cubicle where Kasturi is waiting for him and occupies his chair saying "What is it? You look disturbed; we would have talked over the phone." Kasturi sounds annoyed "Over the phone? We have been talking daily for more than a week now as Francis. I hope you can understand what this dealership means to us. This is the only means we can survive and due to your office's further negligence we will lose this opportunity as well." While she speaks Francis opens his laptop and looks at it and then at Kasturi in between. He responds "I understand, but it is not so easy and will take its own time." Kasturi's voice rises "We don't have time, Taurus Medicare is not going to wait for us and we cannot tell them that it will take its own time. Their finance manager says it is just a matter of 10 days and it should be done. I have been talking to you for the past 8 days with no feedback yet. At least explain why is it going to take time?"

Francis turns the screen of his laptop facing her and shows her pointing at the screen "see we have already

filed Kasturi, not that we are not working on it."
Kasturi looks at the screen, hardly able to understand
what it means. He closes the flab of the laptop and
continues "that is a procedure. We need to file the
case at NCLT, there will be a hearing and since it is
not been filed for two years the company is struck
off. If we need to retrieve the company now we need
to pay a penalty for a total of 5 years. After strike-off
another 3 years passed." Katuri holds her head
uttering "Francis I reminded you several times about
this account block. I was not even aware of this
strike-off thing. It is my mistake; being Director of a
Pvt.Ltd company I should have known all this.
Francis tries to calm her "Don't worry, I am trying."
Kasturi is still furious at him "Why did you not do it
when I was even reminding you" she is on the verge
of crying. Francis defends himself "Sit, I will explain."
He continues "it was two years default and the
penalty for that is heavy. It is per day Rs.350/- so
now if we calculate it is going to be in lacs. Do we
have that amount to pay?" Kasturi cuts him in-
between "But, you should have done that time itself
when the account was blocked." Francis explains,
"There was a notification expected from the
Government that struck off companies need not go
to NCLT rather it can be managed at ROC level
which would be easier then. I was waiting for that
notification." "Waiting for notification for 3years
Francis? Look where we stand now. So what's next?"
she questions. "We have to file our case with NCLT"
he responds "our case will come on board and be
heard." "So what about the penalty?" she questions
further. Francis nodes "one good thing is that

currently, Government has given relaxation that if we file at NCLT before 31st december penalty will be waived off and only Rs.10000/- per year would be payable, which accounts to just Rs.50000/- in our case." Kasturi reacts with raised eyebrows without saying anything and Francis understands the unsaid mention that currently Rs.50000/- is not a 'just' for them.

Francis wants her to relax and leave but his assurance that he will file before the end of the day is not working out for Kasturi. She insists and gets the filing done. He checks up with her "who will present the case in front of NCLT? "Kasturi asks "what are the options? Do we need to hire a lawyer?

Francis replies "Yes, we can hire a lawyer. Why don't you do it? You have experienced it too now" he laughs saying so. Kasturi too smiles but doesn't agree with that. She questions suggesting "can you present? In this case, any queries you would be in a better position to reply to, isn't it?

Francis agrees saying that the company can be represented by its Chartered Accountant or Company Secretary. Hence they file it that way. But that is not all about it. Their case has to come on board and that too in time. Soon Kasturi learns that there is a chance that the case is not taken on board before 31st December. She is really surprised to hear from Francis that there is nothing that can be done about it but waits and watches. Clearance from ROC concerning Tax filing is also required. Avinash spends two days meeting officials to find out what the procedure is all about and fetches the contact details from ROC and NCLT as well who can guide them on this. Now it is about following up with these short-listed persons. Kasturi keeps a close watch on updates if their cases are taken on board. Several times calls Francis. There is no further movement from his office. It is not the time to argue with Francis or take his office staff for questioning. She decides to find it out for herself. With the help of Avinashs's information, she reaches the NCLT office.

By the time she reaches NCLT, it is already 1.30pm and the official lunchtime for them. She enquires about the lady who is in charge of their case as mentioned by Avinash. The inquiry counter seems to be very helpful and guides on all queries she has. The concerned lady is on leave but the person at the counter helps her out to find out the exact status of their case. The first level of scrutiny was done, the ROC report was submitted by Francis but he had not yet replied to the queries raised in the scrutiny. She calls him just to check the update available at his end.

Kasturi asks"Hi Francis? What's the status at NCLT? We don't have much time." Francis responds "Yes, I am sitting with our file with my contact at NCLT and will get it sorted out today at any cost." Kasturi reacts "what cost?" Francis responds "Yes, we will need to pay him something to get our file through" Kasturi reacts "pay?" Francis responds "lets see." Kasturi sighs before further questioning "where exactly are you? "Francis senses her questioning and tries to be more appropriate in answering 'I was on the 6th floor, their back office. Just came out as he went for Lunch. I will go back in an hour again."

The next day, Kasturi tries to call NCLT but in vain. The contact number is either busy or unanswered. She again leaves and reaches NCLT around 3 pm. Lucky enough to meet the female handling her file. She has politely warned Francis and he too is there by 3.30 pm. He talks with the lady and gets the reply to the queries uploaded just before they leave for the day.

As decided, Kasturi again tries to call NCLT on Monday morning to check when their case can be taken on board now. Fortunately, this time the phone is answered and they share court officer Aakash contact number with her. This guy holds the file now and is the only contact for further follow-ups.

Kasturi calls Aakash without delay. Aakash doesn't pick up even when she calls again after an hour or so. She is all set to leave for NCLT but just takes a chance if he responds on WhatsApp. She drops a message saying "trying your number. Need to talk about our case which has come to court no.4.

To Kasturis's surprise, he responds 'please call at 5.30 pm'. She feels a bit relieved. He confirms that the File is with him and that he will revert on the date for when the case is taken on board. He sounds confident that it will be done in a day or two. Kasturi is further relieved.

Back home her thoughts continue to search for a way out.

Prakash is her close friend's elder brother and one of the directors of a big firm dealing with Mechanical spares.

Kasturi has known Prakash since her college days and has been talking to him just like an elder brother. He has been guiding her on any business-related matters. It is almost 10.30 pm hence she checks up with her friend before calling him if it was ok to call at this time. Leena says "Look at your problem Kasturi and in this situation, you want to think of this? Just call him. If he is sleeping, he may not pick up but try." Kasturi goes by Leena's suggestion and calls. He doesn't pick up. She is about to lie down and her phone rings. She receives and runs to the terrace to avoid disturbing kids who are fast asleep. "Yes Kasturi, How are you? How are things, and is your matter of getting the dealership sorted?" Have you started working on it?" he enquires. Kasturi briefs him all about the strike-off and the consequences they are facing at this final stage. He patiently hears her and calmly responds "So, if your case is not heard immediately then this dealership is gone and this is the only chance as of now that your business can survive right?"

She utters very slowly "Yes"His piece of advice is just on the point "No one will come to your rescue. You will have to do it yourself. Just get up in the morning, go to NCLT and directly approach the Judge. Put your matter in front of him, tell him that this is the only chance of your survival and he will understand and do whatever is possible". Kasturi listens to Prakash and again asks "But, how can I directly go to the Judge? It may not be possible. No one will allow me to approach him. Prakash reacts "You have nothing to lose if this strike off is not removed you have to shut down your business which I believe is already on the verge of that. In such a situation, you will need to do whatever it takes, else sit calmly and look for a Job to just earn your bread" He disconnects without checking how it felt to her to listen to this. That feeling of the end of the 20 years of hard work which would practically go down the drain just sucks her from within. Prakash's calm but sharp words keep on poking her throughout the night. She sends a message to Francis that she will be visiting NCLT without calling Aakash or anyone else tomorrow.

Early in the morning she gets ready and while on the way she receives a call from Francis. Without giving him a chance to talk she says "I am coming to your office in 15mins you need to join me". She calls him when she reaches close to his office and again without letting him speak she says "waiting down please come fast we need to go " Francis is well aware that she won't listen hence he just says "Ok." She waits for more than 30 mins and he is still not there. She has a feeling that if someone asks some details that she is not able to answer then Francis's presence is needed hence though she senses that he is not keen on joining her as he believes that they need to wait till their case is taken on board but Kasturi doesn't mind his opinion. She calls him till he picks "I have to complete some work before leaving, why don't you come to my office and wait? I will pick you up from there. Kasturi is practically waiting for him on the side of the road and refuses to go to his office. She feels that he may again call up his contact and that may again lead to cancelling the visit.

Francis calls her when it is more than an hour that she is waiting." Where are you? I am at the junction you mentioned" She guides him to reach her, and gets in his car as he halts. Francis picks up his phone and dials a number. Kasturi is a bit furious "Don't call anyone, we are directly going." Francis too sounds a bit angry "there is no point in going without checking. No one will entertain us there." He speaks over the phone in response to whatever is said from the other side "oh, is it so."

Kasturi is not willing to listen but Francis conveys. "Yesterday evening's list also does not mention our case and now it will be done only after Christmas vacation. Kasturi is shocked to hear this "After vacation, that means this chance of penalty waiver is lost and also Taurus Medicare dealership." Tears start rolling down. Francis too feels helpless. Kasturi picks up her phone and calls Aakash. "Good morning Aakash, our case did not appear on yesterday's list and I believe now it would be only after vacation." He replies "you can check up on 2nd Jan."

Kasturi insists "can I come and meet? Is there any

possibility that something can be done? Can I meet the Judge and try to convince him to take my case on board?

Aakash had to agree as she is not willing to give up " ok come but I can't assure you as 'Member' don't meet anyone" She notices the unpleasant expressions of Francis who had just started the vehicle after listening to the conversation.

By the time all this exercise is done it is already 2.30 pm. They reach the 5th floor where all courtrooms are located. Coming out of the elevator, Kasturi looks at the floor lobby which has well-organised sitting arrangements and is fully air-conditioned. But the floor is deserted. They come out of the elevator, not knowing what is to be further done when no one is there to guide. Francis asks her to excuse him for he wanted to go out for some work and join back in 15mins. Francis takes an elevator down and Kasturi moves ahead and occupies one of the chairs in the hope that someone would come whom she can check up on Aakash. The air conditioner temperature is too low making her uncomfortable. Her feet also start shaking in anxiety. She calls Aakash but he is not reachable. Squeezing both her arms and trying to control her anxiety she notices a person comes and stands opposite to the only door present on that floor. She checks up with him for Aakash. He too is a visitor, a Chartered accountant of some company, and has come to collect his order for his case heard last week. Kasturi calculates if her case is heard tomorrow and another week to collect the order still it would be just on time. But there are no signs of this yet. This guy mentions to Kasturi that Aakash would be in court now and may come out only after 4 pm once proceedings are over and hence he may not be reachable. Kasturi Sighs as something she could know for now. She keeps patience and looks around if Francis is back. As it is close to 4 pm now few more people are seen there. Few stand outside the door and few opt to sit on chairs. Much before 4 pm a thin, short guy comes out of the door and speaks to this person waiting and hands over a paper to him, and goes back. Kasturi stands up from her chair trying to speak to this guy but he is very fast to get in. Kasturi learns that he was Aakash and that he received his order. Kasturi peeps inside the door but nothing is seen. She comes back and occupies the same chair. Just in a while, Francis joins back. It is pin-drop silence there though there are at least 12-15 people waiting. Kasturi tells Francis in a very low and soft voice that Aakash is inside, to which Francis just nods.

 It is already 4.15 pm and Aakash comes out straight and walks towards Kasturi, she stands up in surprise not expecting this.

"I noticed you when I came out sometimes back madam. I checked up with sir but nothing can be done now." He is about to leave. Kasturi is almost in tears and sounds so as well "is he still there? Please, let me meet him. You know it is a do or die situation for us." Aakash confirms that the Member is in his chamber but won't meet anyone there. She doesn't understand who this member is and continues requesting "please let me meet the Judge, at the most he will be angry and refuse to talk, and I am ok even if he scolds me." Aakash feels a little bad for her and says "Don't cry madam, I will try asking him." Kasturi doesn't notice but her eyes are already pouring. He goes in and comes out within no time. Aakash sounds helpless while mentioning to her "Member refused to meet. They won't meet anyone, I told you."

Kasturi "I want to meet the Judge, who is Member" She feels a bit awkward to know that the Judge is addressed as 'the Member' as she was not aware of this.

Looking at her sad face Aakash whispers "Member will leave in some time. You can try talking to him while he passes through the lobby or waits for the elevator. "Kasturi nods with hope and looking at this one chance responds"ok."

After another half-hour's wait, a tall fair person walks out of the door walking through the lobby followed by Aakash and a couple of other persons. They wait for the elevator and Kasturi is quick to get up and approach him, she hears Francis saying "No Kasturi" from behind but who cares. She is already in front of this tall man, "The Judge" for her and "The Member "for Aakash. She is polite as ever "Sir, my case is not taken on board yet. It is very crucial for us else my business will shut down. Please help." He looks at her as she speaks and then at Aakash "Check and see what can be done for her case"and they all enter the elevator.

Kasturi comes toward Francis who still has a big question mark on his face for what she had just done.

Aakash comes back from the elevator and enters that door. Before she can think if he is ignoring her, he comes to Kasturi and conveys "I have taken your case onboard for tomorrow" and turns back going towards the door. She runs behind asking "What time should we come then?"

Aakash responds "It will be heard online. Before the end of the day I will add you to the WhatsApp group of companies in tomorrow's list and the link will be shared on that group. You will need to join using that link." Kasturi expresses her gratitude as he leaves and turns around to almost dash with Francis who is also standing behind her as she talks.

As decided she reaches Francis's office at 10am sharp but doesn't react when he turns out at 11.15am, making her wait for more than an hour. He arrives and is cool, behaving as if no big deal in being late. Her thoughts are boiling, recollecting the sequence of episodes she had to go through due to his and his office's negligence. She just keeps the boiling point under control. They log in by 11.30 with the help of a link shared on the group she was added to last night. Their company name appeared 20th on the list and by the time they log in the 7th case is on board. Both her fists cover her crossed fingers. It is 1.30 pm and the court breaks for lunch in the middle of the 14th case.

Resuming back from Lunchtime court continues with the ongoing case. It is 4.30 pm when the Judge gives them a further date going on to the 15th case. It is just 30mins more before the court would call off the day. Francis says "Our type of cases will not even take 5mins, it will be done don't worry. Kasturi is under the impression that the court is bound to complete the declared list for the day but it is only at the end of the timing she realises when the court calls off for the day after hearing the 18th case that it is not so. She is not yet aware of what would happen further. She calls Aakash, as expected he doesn't pick but by 9.30 pm or so he posts a list for the next day. Kasturi holds her head noticing their turn to be 41st now. With listing on 20th no. their turn didn't come now at 41st looks like a faraway chance.

The second day goes more than anxious when the court closes hearing 28 cases for the day. The third-day list is posted and they are on the 56th number now. Kasturi gallops her suffocation before leaving Francis's office.

Kasturi reaches around 11.30am on the third day. It is the 12th case of the day going on then. There are queries raised on the WhatsApp group as many companies and their representatives are unaware of the procedures for many first-timers like Kasturi. Checking chats in between the talks she discovers that it is the last day of court today. Judge is going on leave before Christmas vacation and the court will further resume only on the 2nd now. Hope is getting low and so is Kasturi's face.

There's just an hour left now by the time the 30th case ends. Another 25 more cases are to be heard before their turn. It looks impossible and there is a sudden murmur on screen. Kasturi is not able to understand what's going on. Francis picks up his hands-free and tries to concentrate. He removes his hand's free earphones and with a relieved expression tells Kasturi with thumbs up "Today being the last day, the Judge has asked to present only Strike-off cases now. Still not knowing if they would be heard today she silently sends a WhatsApp message to Aakash "Ours is the 56th number, will it be done today?" The reply is not expected but flashes in the notification of her phone instantly "Yes' '. Her fingers feel relaxed as the fists open to join her hands together saying "Thank God." In less than 20mins it is their turn. Francis briefs in front of 'The Member', "ROC filing was missed and even the notices for some reason. He also shares his screen showing GST and other filings are compiled and requests for the retrieval of the company as there is good scope for the business to continue." Female Member (Judge) who has logged in from her residence responds "Permitted with charges of Rs.10000/- per annum accounting to Rs.50000/- In total. Pay before the due date else this order stands cancelled."

Francis has to complete some more paperwork and collect the order copy the next day.

Kasturi doesn't fail to call and thank Prakash for pushing her to take charge of the situation. He too mentions that being a little blunt was required as he wanted her to address the issues in any possible way.

Kasturi recollects the person who was there to collect his order after a week. She again drops the message to Aakash if she can collect the order and he responds that it would take another two days at least. By this time Kasturi contacts Anjali and her boss to convey that the strick-off is removed. He replies that it should appear on the ROC site before 31st Dec else he will not be able to hold on.

Aakash shares a mail id of NCLT on her WhatsApp "send mail on this email id requesting a certified copy of order." She does it instantly as it is already 25th by now. Leaves a day in between and again calls NCLT on 27th just to know that the order is yet to be signed.

It is the 28th, she reaches the NCLT office. A normal calm view at the reception is missing and there is absolute chaos today. Every one of these 25-30 people is shouting at this person at reception whom she has always found to be more than helpful. She calls Francis and he says he is already started. Failing to understand, what's going on Kasturi asks one of the persons there. At the peak of his voice he expresses "It is been 15days and they are not giving order copy to us. If today we don't submit it in ROC we will not be able to get the benefit of penalty waiver and today they are saying Registrar is gone to Calcutta and will be back only on 2nd."Kasturi's gets tensed hearing this; she rests herself on the chair behind her in a reflex action. Not knowing what is to be done now, she approaches the reception passing through this crowd. She looks at this guy through the glass window. Looking at her he speaks "Madam, what can we do if "Member" is not there. We can just convey it to you all." Pretending to be calm she asks "None of the orders is signed, 16th also?" He responds "Yes Madam, staff does their work on time but if they don't sign, what can we do?" Kasturi asks further "But, we need to submit the signed copy at ROC else the whole exercise is waste, is there any other option?" By the time he could respond to her the crowd had just come from behind and Kasturi has to come out of it with difficulty. She calls Francis, briefing him which is of no use. Avinash is in touch while working in Kolhapur and knew she would not leave a single stone unturned.

She sits for a while thinking of all that would follow if this order is not submitted at ROC. She requests one of the officials to at least issue an order without certifying but that too is out of scope for this staff. Someone mentions that it will be uploaded on the NCLT site. She tries to checkup on her phone but the weak signal doesn't allow her to do so. Avinash suggests that he can download and mail her and she can get the printout of the copy from a nearby shop. She comes down and looks for the stationery shop, takes a couple of copies of this uncertified order copy, and just rushes to the ROC office. She checks up with Francis who is still on the way past 2hrs for this 30mins distance, if he has any contact in ROC but he conveys that, that level of contact won't work at this stage and still give her the name of that person.

She takes a Taxi and reaches ROC. Looking for this person kills another 15-20mins and she learns that this guy left for the day post lunch due to personal reasons. Kasturi looks for the nameplates on each Cabin and notices a board Asst. Commissioner, Jadhav. She hangs out of his cabin for some time giving it a thought if she should directly enter. When she is about to do so, someone shouts at her from behind "Madam wait, what is it?" She replies "I want to meet Mr.Jadhav."

He checks with her "Do you have an appointment." Kasturi replies "No, but it is urgent. If I won't be able to meet him today my company is finished." He senses tension in her voice and asks her to sit on the chair outside the cabin. She has no option but to follow. She waits for more than an hour and he is yet to consider her request to let her in. Kasturi keeps on watching the activities in the cabin through the glass door while this peon keeps on roaming through the corridor, in Jadhav's cabin and out, each time assuring her that Jadhav is busy and he will check up if she can see him once he is free. Getting anxious about overrunning time she sits in an alert position as two ladies enter Jadhav's cabin and she rushes in as they come out noticing that Jadhav is following them. She is in front of Jadhav saying "sorry to come without an appointment sir, but I have no option. It is urgent." He replies "wait, I will be back in some time." He leaves and she is back in her seat. It is already 4.30pm when she checks up with a person sitting next to her for what time does the office close. He replies "5.30 pm madam." There is a brief chat between Kasturi and this man who mentions that he is watching her for a long. He is curious to know about Kasturi and enquires "Are you a Company secretary" Kasturi replies "No, I am the director of the company." He further asks "Your CA is not with you?" She responds "No, it was urgent hence I came myself."

Jadhav enters his cabin when it is just 15mins for the office to close. She stands up and walks towards the cabin. Peon comes and stands in between her and the cabin door saying "wait." He enters and comes out in no time permitting her to go in.

Jadhav offers her to sit and offers a glass of water as her anxiety drips from her face. She holds the glass of water and is speechless with a dry throat and wet eyes. He repeats "Have some water you will be able to speak then." She takes a sip and briefs all about her company strike off and consequences and dealership etc till she landed up in front of his cabin. Jadhav sounds helpful as he enquires about her qualification and business "so, you must be earning a lot in this business, isn't it." Kasturi senses his expectation "Sir, not really, and currently it is a matter of retrieving our company just to survive." He opens up Rs.15,000/- and explains "As per protocol, we need a certified copy of the order as companies and their CAs cheat sometimes but you look genuine and I will anyway cross verify from NCLT before uploading your order." Kasturi mentions "Sir, but I am not carrying that much cash." Jadhav says "Yes, of course." Where is your CA? He has to do all this that you are doing. Call him and he can get the amount. Meantime you go downstairs and submit this order copy. It has to be entered in an inward register and after that, it will come to me. Ask Bhoir to get this letter to me immediately after the entry." He looks at the wall clock on the right side and tells Kasturi to rush as it is already time to close the inward counter. She rushes saying "ok sir, Thank you."

Downstairs at the counter, the lady is about to leave. Kasturi quickly makes a call to Francis and asks him to come with the cash. Francis, who is on the way to NCLT since early afternoon, immediately agrees "I will withdraw cash and reach.

The lady at inward counter politely says as Kasturi approaches her "Madam, I have just locked my drawer. Please come tomorrow morning. Kasturi requests "Madam just two minutes, sir has asked to make the entry and give him this order immediately." Lady is in no mood to help "Madam, I will miss my train" and she leaves saying "Meet Bhoir, he will be here around." Another 5mins and Bhoir is there explaining that, since the lady left for the day this order can be entered only the next day. He is helpful indeed and agrees to keep the copy with him and that he will get it done the next day and Kasturi need not come again. She has no option but to agree with thanks.

She walks out of the campus and calls Francis again. He is there in the next 20 mins. They both go to Jadhav's cabin. He too is about to leave. Francis greets him before handing over a packet "Sir, I could manage to get only Rs.10000/- from the ATM." Not uttering anything Jadhav looks at Kasturi and she covers it up saying "ok, sir, can we send the balance by tomorrow morning?" Jadhav agrees. Kasturi tells him that she couldn't get the order Inwarded and that Bhoir will do the needful tomorrow morning.

Jadhav guides further "enclose a letter with that requesting to remove the strike-off. It has to be typed so rush and get the letter typed else they will also close soon." Jadhav looks at Francis "You are her CA, right? You should be doing this running around what she is doing." Francis tries to defend himself "I was doing some important documentation for her so…"

Finding the shop for taking a printout, mailing a draft letter on its id, and taking print kills another half hour but it is done after Kasturi has to practically run to reach in time and they hand over the letter to Bhoir. They again meet Jadhav and inform him that it is done. He assures that he will clear the strike-off status once the order copy comes to him and also the balance amount of course goes unmentioned though.

The next day Kasturi keeps on checking the status and by afternoon sends a message to Jadhav that it is still not done. He replies "working on it"

The next day again she checks with him and He asks for the company Name and confirms "It is done, Madam."

Strike—off was cleared a day before the so-called

deadline of 31st December. But that was not all; another Government office was waiting to welcome Kasturi.

Before they could get the feeling that the paperwork is through now, Avinash sends a screenshot of mail he received from Taurus Medicare. It mentioned another query regarding their Drug Licence. Their company was Pvt. ltd but their Drug Licence missed this which they had never noticed. Their existing business had no requirement for Drug Licence but Avinash had foreseen the possibility of expansion and got it done through some Known person. They were happy as it was Taurus Medicare's requirement and they already had it. It was not in regular use and hence the incomplete name of the company went unnoticed.

Avinash is out of town and it is last day of the year. They have this one day to submit the amended copy of the drug licence. Avinash guides her and she reaches the drug office just to know that they have shifted to another location. She rushes to that new location. Not knowing whom exactly to approach, she enters a room and the lady in there looks like a helpful female. But to Kasturi's surprise, she shouts at her saying "I cannot look after everything. How come you are asking me about the amendment and that too on this year-end day when half of the staff is on leave and out of Mumbai for celebration?"

This lady scribbles a mobile number on a small piece of paper and hands it over to Kasturi "Contact him on this number, he will guide you. Kasturi is not able to understand if the lady was trying to help or get rid of her. Whatever the situation, she has helped with contact number.

Kasturi comes out of the cabin dialling the given number, and it gets connected immediately "

"Mr.Bhosle, I am Kasturi and need to amend my company name on the drug licence" Bhosle is casual in his response "ok madam, you can meet me in my office on 4th January." Kasturi sounds worried "4th January sir? It would be too late sir. I need to submit this amended copy to the company offering us a dealership before the end of the day else we lose our chance of survival. Sir, we are facing lots of problems for so many years and if this opportunity is lost we will have to shut down our business. Please help sir "Just before completing her request in a single breath she closes her eyes as she feels too bad for she thinks she sounded too desperate. Bhosle doesn't react much, just conveys that Deputy Commissioner Rao is out of office for a meeting and may or may not even come back for the day. Still, he asks her to give him a call around 4 pm.

Feeling a little discouraged, Kasturi takes an auto-rickshaw, calls Avinash and conveys that it may not be possible to get the drug licence amended today. While talking to Avinash she hears a beep of a call waiting on her phone and its Bhosle's number. She disconnects Avinash's call and takes his call. Bhosle asks her to come to his office immediately as Rao is expected any moment for some small work and then he will immediately leave to join his on-going meeting at their head office hence she can take a chance to meet him. She requests the auto-rickshaw guy to immediately take a U-turn and drop her back at the same place. She rushes into the building where the drug licence office is situated. It takes a bit of exercise to finally reach Bhosle's cabin. He is the only person in the entire office. Kasturi guessed that it must be lunchtime.

Bhosle offers her a seat and a glass of water. He opens the official website to check the application form which they had submitted while applying for a drug licence. He notices that there was a mistake from either side which resulted in the incomplete name of the company appearing on the drug licence. He files the amendment form and keeps the rest of the documents ready for Rao to sign. It is almost 4.30 pm but no sign of Rao yet. Bhosle walks out of his office and calls Kasturi on her number within 10mins "Madam, sir won't come today. You can leave. He will be signing only on the 4th." There is not much scope for her to say anything. She knew how crucial it is to get the drug licence amended but she is helpless and had no option but to leave. Coming out of that building she walks towards the auto-rickshaw stand, her phone is in her hand she looks at it and dials Bhosle's number "Sir, can you share Mr.Rao's number I will just try talking to him." Bhosle readily shares his number as he witnessed her restlessness while she sat across the table.

Fingers crossed and she calls Rao, "Sir, I am here at

your office needing your signature for we applied for a name amendment on our drug licence. With no hope and no go, she briefs her situation to him. To her surprise, Rao responds positively "You wait upstairs I will be there in half an hour." Upstairs Bhosle is about to leave his office but stays back as Kasturi briefs about her call with Rao.

Rao is in his cabin within 15 mins and immediately asks his office boy to get Kasturi's documents. In no time her documents are signed and handed over to her. She is not able to believe it as she is under the impression that once Rao comes he will take his own sweet time to sign.

How could she leave without expressing her gratitude to Rao? He too comments "Madam, Government employees are unnecessarily ill-famed if any work is delayed. Now you should share this experience.

 Finally, documentation compliance is achieved in time.

Expect the Unexpected

It is been 5years since they had purchased this plot at Khopoli. For one or the other reason, there was not even a thought of any construction there. Solving house matter and then facing the business downfall landed Avinash and Kasturi into only paying the maintenance for this place without utilising it.

Now that the strike-off is removed, Kastri informs Anjali and her boss about the same. It is the beginning of the year and Anjali had already conveyed to Kasturi that till the 10th of Jan they cannot expect anything as everyone would be busy with yearly closure and further paperwork.

The Challenge of arranging funds still prevailed as lockdown had practically paused Avinash's Cairo project.

Where initial discussion begins with arranging 15 lacs and they have already raised this amount from whatever business exists. It is almost a year since the talks started and by this time all documentation is through but lots has changed and the same business demands 45-50 lacs now.

She visits the bank for any possible options. Shantanu is as helpful as ever. He assures that he can get the business loan done and also convinces the Branch Manager to consider but it is only 10 lacs that could get sanctioned where Kasturi requests for 50 lacs.

Avinash proposes to sell off their current bungalow and start everything back from the stretch. Probably, this is the only possibility remaining. Arranging another 40 lacs is highly impossible. Their bankers had done their bit with full support as Shantanu had seen company finances while business was at peak but the past performance is not going to help currently.

Kasturi regularly follows up with Sudesh if he can arrange some funds. She learns lots of options for raising funds like using someone else's property but the interest to be paid would leave them with no profit. Moreover, both of them are not convinced for this option. Kasturi thinks, can our own house be used similarly and checks the same with Shantanu again and he is not very happy to convey that due to drop in their business in the past two years this will not be possible.

Ramesh from the finance company who gave LAP just makes a casual call as usual enquiring if their EMIs are regular and if the business has been affected due to lockdown. He is aware that due to the on-going Pandemic and consequent lockdown, they have taken the benefit of moratorium as declared by Government but that has only addressed the problem of today. Casual talks leads to Kasturi's query "Ramesh, we have two properties one is already mortgaged with your firm and another place at Khopoli. Can you not help us to get funds using this Khopoli place? You are working for a financing firm;

you may be able to guide us on this."

Ramesh promises to get back if any possibility strikes him. Kasturi also calls Shantanu, mentioning looking for any possibility wherein they can use the Khopoli plot. Shantanu enquires about the plot cost, and location and conveys that no bank will consider undeveloped land. According to Shantanu, if the land value is 60 lacs and even if small construction worth 4-5 lacs is constructed with RCC slab then the land cost plus construction cost put together can be considered but just land will be zero value as for Bank guarantee or Loan against property is to be considered by the bank. Again this is possible if and only if we can show a fair amount of business for at least 6 months. Kasturi's argument that how can we show business before you fund us, carries no value here.

Kasturi discusses the possibilities from Shantanu with Avinash. Not finding any way out they decide to give it a thought to go ahead with minimal construction at Khopoli.

It is almost mid January and only two months left for arranging funds. Kasturi thanked Anjali for deciding in March to take over from the existing dealer. Avinash makes several visits to Khopoli and shortlists local contractors who almost have a monopoly in this area. Hence, there is no second option. Considering their plot size contractor presents the option of a big and luxurious bungalow. But while finalising they mention to him exactly the purpose of this construction, their limited budget, and time constraint. He promises to hand over the completed structure not only with all electrical and plumbing fittings but also with all permissions for construction, the electric meter in not more than 45days. He is not willing to take the responsibility of permission from the Collector's office as it is not feasible for him. He insists that he will go ahead with construction work with local authority permission and by the time construction is completed they can complete the formalities from the Collector office. He doesn't forget to mention that many of the constructions are not even going for Collector office permission. The first advance for the construction is given but Avinash warns the contractor that this construction should be started only post permission from the collector office.

It is arranging the funds now for the construction too. Not very fond of ornaments, Kasturi had very minimal gold and they opted for a gold loan which is hardly 50% of the construction cost. Rest again adds to the challenge list with the many other participants of the list still unknown.

Kasturi and Avinash reach the collector office at Alibaug just at lunchtime. One office boy directs them to Garud who briefs on the procedure and in turn directs to the xerox shop for collecting the form and submitting it after duly filling it. They come out of the office, look for the shop and collect the forms. Avinash is already carrying all the relevant documents which he could figure out. They fill the form with the help of the girl working at the xerox shop, encloses documents, and enjoys the tasty treat of a household meal at the adjacent restaurant while waiting for Garud to come back from Lunch.

Papers are submitted successfully. Gund guides them to come next week and take documents to the Town planner (TP) office and Kasturi does so in the interest of speeding up the process. Paresh, assistant to the TP commissioner guides her appropriately during her consecutive visits to the TP office. Everyone seems to be very helpful. As said, things happen only when it is destined to happen. Not only is the Architect's plan submitted is not as per the guidelines but she is also required to submit the Land survey Map which needs to be fetched from the Tehsildar office.

It is another exercise to get the Land survey map. It not only takes several visits but even several months just to know that the office is not even able to find the copy in their office. The staff there would make her wait for the entire day in the name of searching for it and eventually one fine day they disclose that the office doesn't have the copy.

Not bothering about the consequence, Kasturi blasts the concerned person when he mentions that the measurements will need to be taken again and the map needs to be made. It is going to involve the society of 350 members who would not cooperate as it is not their requirement and it is going to be time consuming too. All this is just because they don't have the copy. One of the office boys mentions to

Kasturi that the original owner or the developer may have one copy and that would be easy for her rather than visiting this office. She contacts the society office and developer office and finally can trace it at the office of the original property owner. They do share the scan copy and Kasturi is finally able to get the Map duly signed and stamped from the Tehsil office but not before giving them one copy as well.

The TP commissioner, Mr.Bhagat is also a very helpful person. He calls Kasturi and asks her to take the architect on-line. Talking to the architect Mr.Bhagat gets annoyed as he seems to understand nothing and just keeps repeating that he has made the drawing according to the latest guidelines. Too much annoyed by his lack of understanding Mr.Bhagat disconnects the phone. The architect believes that the Town Planner office will not clear her documents unless their monitory requirement is addressed but Kasturi doesn't feel so. She calls back Mr.Bhagat and to her surprise, he offers to help her saying, I will get it done here madam you just pay the scrutiny fees of Rs.600/-. She pays the same and Paresh organises a copy after charging some extra amount of course.

It is all clear from Taurus Medicare now and they get a go-ahead for signing the dealership agreement. But, there is still a big question mark yet, FUNDS? With all their attempts to find a way out still ON, there is nothing concrete in hand yet. The situation looks like they will have to back off from the dealership due to a lack of funds. That would be the worst part ever.

Kasturi happens to visit a small school of underprivileged kids near her office premises every week and teach Maths and Science to the kids of 8th and 9th grade. This Sunday it is a meeting at the office with the Principal, Mrs.Agarwal who admires Kasturi for taking out time for teaching from her busy schedule. She notices Kasturi is lost in her thoughts today and leaves the meeting early giving an excuse for some personal work.

Mrs Agarwal in her mid-fifties has been working here as a Principal for many years now. Knowledgeable in most matters. You ask her and she is ready with the solutions for one and all issues that pop up.

Kasturi receives a call from Mrs.Agarwal just as she reaches her house. She thinks it was not right on her part to leave the meeting and hence this call is to enquire. She is right, Mrs.Agarwal in her soft voice asks her "What's the matter, dear? I have been noticing this for a couple of months; you seem to be carrying some tension. Is it so? Is everything alright? Where is Avinash? Travelling?" Kasturi replies "no, he is in Mumbai"

Mrs.Agarwal further enquires"what's the matter then? You can share if you feel so." Kasturi responds "It is just a business matter Mrs.Agarwal nothing else." Mrs.Agarwal tries to convince "If you feel you can share. Business always goes up and down. Today there is some problem; tomorrow it will be resolved for sure. All days are not the same you see."

Kasturi is on the verge of crying because her problem

is big and hesitates to mention it to her. She doesn't respond much as her throat is heavy by now. Just say "Hmm." Mrs Agarwal hangs up saying "don't worry and take care, if I can do anything let me know."

Kasturi's thoughts keep on wandering as always suggesting that she should share her requirement with Mrs.Agarwal, maybe she can help her find some way out. By late afternoon she calls her back "Hello madam, good evening." Her voice is heavy and Mrs.Agarwal understands this and calmly asks "yes, tell me. Look, you should share your problems, only then can someone help find some way out." Kasturi responds "yes" and briefs her all about from Femys Creations to Taurus Medicare dealership option, their options to raise funds or Bank Guarantee, Khopoli options, etc, and that if this opportunity is lost it is going to be more than a problem.

Mrs.Agarwal patiently listens, ending the conversation by saying "Don't worry; something will work out for sure. I have seen you both are hard working. Things will get sorted out. After a brief conversation, she hangs up saying if she can come to school around 11.30 am

Mrs.Agarwal relaxes on the couch in her cabin while Kasturi pulls a chair. They discuss school matters. She takes out a bunch of papers from him big paper bag and hands them over to Kasturi as she says "this is my LIC policy document worth Rs.1800000/- I can take this and add another 2 lacs and give it to you. Will it be sufficient enough to solve your problem?

Kasturi looks at her with wet eyes as she continues "whatever I get from LIC you pay that interest. You can return once your arrangements are done." Kasturi is not able to believe. What she was trying hard for and there was no way to get this amount, it had just come to the doorstep from where it was not expected at all. Kasturi is so touched by the helping hand lent by Mrs.Agarwal that she is not even able to express her gratitude to her. She is just speechless.

Back home at the end of the day, Kasturi stands in front of Sai's idol, her heart says "when I feel it is time to give up, you hold it on to prove your point that giving up is never an option!"

It is time for Avinash's Cairo project to take off. All through the lockdown he has been working on sourcing, finalising, and making payments to the vendors. He had already ordered machines from their regular supplier from the USA but delays due to lockdown, and increased freights are going to substantially reduce the profit margin of this project. Kasturi wants to take a chance as always to try and further negotiate for machines.

Liam, one of the partners of the company, also happens to be Kasturi's Facebook friend. He is fond of Kasturi's younger son since they met at Kasturi's house over dinner while he visited India. He had expressed many times that he felt he was just like Varun as a kid. Liam used to imitate Donald Ducks' voice and hence Varun always addressed him as Donald Uncle.

With the thought that if at all they can get some discount on regular costs then they can return Mrs.Agarwal's money, Kasturi initiates talks with Liam. She sends him a message on Facebook messenger requesting a convenient time to talk and he responds immediately with a return call. He looked after European countries and technically India was not his region but he reverts that he will speak with his team.

It is a regular talk for more than a week and she gets a fair bargain. Liam manages to convince his team as both the companies shared a fair repo past more than 18years.

Liam also proposes to have a joint venture between both companies. This proposal was worked out a few years back as well but couldn't take off for some reason. Liam feels that would have been not the right time hence it didn't happen and that now he will personally look into it.

Kasturi spots another ray of hope.

This is by all means in their favour as Liam proposes to invest and expects technical expertise from Kasturi and Avinash. With this project on board, they would find a way to recover from their business and finance downfall. They discuss lots over calls. Options are exchanged and zeroed down to the workable proposal. Liam expresses his willingness to travel to India for finalising once the lockdown is completely released. It is just the wait till then. Kasturi wants to mention this to Avinash but decides to hold on till

Liam confirms his visit.

Where lockdown takes further toll on the business, Kasturi keeps following up with the TP office. Delays due to many of the employees being covid positive are more than bothering.

Kasturi posts Varun's reels on Facebook and like many of her friends Liam too is a prompt replier. He appreciates Varun's dance and also mentions that he is looking forward to watching it in person soon while he visits to finalise the proposal. Kasturi is desperately looking forward to his visit of course for it is going to be a new beginning altogether. Next two days Kasturi is in a dilemma if she should call him or wait for him to respond?

A day pass and it is Sunday. Kasturi decides to speak with Liam the next day if he doesn't revert by himself on the proposal. Kasturi comes home after a giggly chat with her friends. She sips some water standing in the balcony.With one hand holding a glass of water and the other scroll Facebook posts.

She is hardly able to express to the rest of the world what this post means to her as she reads "with a heavy heart I am shattered. My kind, smart loving brother Liam passed away unexpectedly."

With Liam, all those plans and that ray of hope gets buried forever. Kasturi is moved by the news but her eyes are dry and she is not able to express anything. Just sits down on the nearby chair and keeps reading all posts expressing their feelings.

Final talks are expected to be concluded with Taurus and the agreement is to be signed by both the companies. The formality of Trace certification is completed. Work begins without formal training as there still are travel restrictions but their team takes over the new work comfortably.

Though Mrs.Agarwal lends 20 lacs there is another 20-30 lacs requirement. Kasturi doesn't hesitate this time and requests Mrs.Agarwal for another 20 lacs if possible. She is happy to help. But this is not all. These amounts are attracting 13% interest and are just able to hold on to the dealership of Taurus Medicare for them. Unless these amounts are returned the picture is going to be just good enough to look at.

Beginning of Khopoli Construction is yet to start for the want of formal permission from the collector office and other documentations are taking longer than expected.

Further talks with Ramesh reveals that since the finance company is a non-banking firm they will not be able to do anything on bank guarantee. Kasturi visits her bankers and talks to Shantanu, if they can take over their Loan against property (LAP) from the finance company and then issue a Bank guarantee against the difference between LAP and the actual value of the property. Shantanu is not sure if this can be done as it is not only about the value of the bungalow but also the performance of the company and the credibility will only depend on the returns filed for the past two years, which is not attractive at present.

Kasturi insists that he should try it out. Shantanu is not keen on considering this fearing the rejection of the proposal. She feels this is the only way out for now and despite Shantanu's discouragement she convinces him to at least allow her to meet the Branch Manager and if it is 'no' from her she would not insist. Shantanu checks up with Mrs.Bhatia, the branch manager and accompanies Kasturi to her cabin. Graceful Mrs. Bhatia greets Kasturi and offers her a seat "yes madam, Shantanu mentioned your request"and before Mrs.Bhatia could say anything further Kasturi begins "Madam, we are facing challenges in our business for the past couple of years. We have been banking with you since the conception of this company hence I want to request you to please consider taking over our LAP and help us with Bank Guarantee as well. This is the only property with us but it is a prime property and would suffice your requirement, with your support we can stand up again." Kasturi is not willing to stop and continues "many so-called big shots borrow so much money from banks and just leave the country leaving all of us to just witness their mess on news channels and small-time entrepreneurs like us have to suffer for no help from banks. It is not fair madam."

Shantanu, who was not in favour outside the cabin turns to be the one seconding Kasturi's option and wholeheartedly briefs all about the company and its growth and record. He repeats all that Kasturi mentioned to him. His sincere attempt doesn't go unnoticed by Kasturi. Mrs.Bhatia agrees with the mention "Madam, you came up with this option and I promise you if there is even 1% chance we will try our level best to make this happen." She instructs Shantanu to initiate the process immediately. More than Kasturi, Shantanu's face lit up with the hope of helping her out.

Shantanu wastes no time and calls his colleague to take over the case. This team is as helpful as Shantanu. Everyone puts their heart into this case courtesy Shantanu's instructions.

Kasturi calls Ramesh when it is time for final disbursement. He is not in the position to believe and tries to convince her to be with hs firm atleast for another six months. But, there is no reason for this now. The moratorium has escalated the balance amount to much more value. Loan take over is going to give the benefit of a few years in loan tenure and 3% on the interest rate.

It is time for Avinash to leave for Cairo. He signs the loan agreement documents along with Kasturi on the day he has to take a flight.

That night Kasturi moves all over her house, touching and feeling all walls and recollecting how she asked it to prove itself this house was not unlucky for them. She feels strong emotions for this place.

Though most of the paperwork is done from the TP office it takes another 4 months for their report and

NOC to reach the collector office; courtesy lockdown, change of the TP officer twice in this small course for reasons not known to Kasturi. Only on receipt of their NOC, do they convey to her that they also need a report from the Tehsil office. She had visited Tehsil office for several months for a Land survey map; she would have got it done had they mentioned this prior. It is almost a year now since she applied for permission. But no arguments, it is not going to favour her in any way. A few more days, a few more visits again to Tehsil office just to know that they have sent the documents for verification in the first month itself to the Talathi office, which is just across the river adjacent to their plot. She follows up with Talathi's office now. It takes her   three visits and the site inspection is done. Talathi's office In turn sends her file to Tehsil which takes another month for no reason she feels. Kasturi is mentally tired of these follow-ups and sends her office boy to Tehsil's office for the final signature is yet to be done before they send her file to the Collector's office.

The office boy is not able to get much information. Vivek, who holds her file, now informs him that Kasturi will need to come personally and immediately the next day she is there. Kasturi approaches Vivek and unlike over the phone, he seems to be not so helpful. He directs Kasturi to Madhu, his other associate. Kasturi meets Madhu requesting "sir my file is with you. Vivek asked me to meet you." She gives him all the relevant details of the file for him to trace it. He looks for the file on the table and it is just there. Kasturi feels he knows and just pretends to search for it. He opens the file and looks for document compliance. She knew her file doesn't lack any documents now. Looking at the body language of Madhu she understands that he is not willing to sign for some reason. She too just stands in front without uttering anything while he holds the file. He is not able to put up his request nor does she show any sign of understanding his unsaid monetary demand. He picks up the pen lying beside, signs it showing unwillingness to do so and mentions "I have signed but both sirs are not in office so your work will not be done today. He hands over the file to her continuing "Vivek too has not signed it." She takes the file and places it in front of Vivek "your sign is to be done, Madhu says." He too depicts the same gesture as Madhu before signing it. He points towards the cabin opposite to his table "Sir, will need to sign before it goes to the Tahsildar. Kasturi looks at the empty cabin "Thanks Vivek, when will sir come? What next?"

Madhu has already informed her that both sirs are not there today but to her surprise Vivek conveys otherwise "He is just around, wait outside the cabin he will come." Kasturi is curious to know more now "and Tehsildar is not there today?" Vivek replies "He too is here but you need to take Rathod sir's signature first" She is happy to know this thinking her work may be completed today. Rathod takes quite a long time to come to his cabin but meets her immediately. Kasturi hands over the file to Rathod. He enquires "which place is it?" She briefs him on the details while his office boy comes in with the bunch of files and they both get into their work-related discussions. Kasturi stands in a hope that .Rathod would sign it in between their discussion but as he doesn't, she interrupts "sir, your signature is required." He looks at the file and then at her "I will have to go through all papers, I need some time." She thinks he will call her some other day but he asks her to sit out for half an hour and that he will check it and call her.

Kasturi waits out with many other people waiting like her. It is just 20 mins that she comes out and Rathod leaves his cabin. She rushes inside and on her inquiry, Vivek mentions that he is gone for lunch and will be back soon. 'Soon' is not less than one and a half hours and Kasturi enters his cabin just behind him saying "sir, my file." Rathod looks at it "yes, sit." She occupies the chair and repeats herself mentioning all details again. Rathod surfs across the file and enquires about her business, qualification etc. and calls Vivek. He checks with Vivek for why he has not enclosed a report to this file to which Vivek mentions that he was waiting for .Rathod's confirmation if there is any shortcoming in the file. Rathod checks him "you and Madhu signed right? All documents are intact. Enclose the report and send it to Tehsildar for final signature. Rathod's unexpressed anger on Vivek for not carrying out work as expected shows that he understands the on-purpose delay from Vivek for an unjustified reason. Kasturi follows Vivek as he walks out of Mr.Rathod's cabin. Vivek again guides her to wait out by the time he will need to prepare the report, enclose it and send it to Tehsildar's office.

Waiting seems endless today. She checks with the peon sitting out of Tahsildar's office if she can meet him. Peon is helpful and asks her to wait for some time and that he will check up if his sir is a bit free. Shortly, he allows her in. This Cabin looks very different from the rest cabins; it is almost like a courtroom. Kasturi stands in front of Tahsildar as he checks her file, he assures her that he will go through it and sign before the end of the day and he insists that there is no need to wait and she can leave. She informs Vivek and also requests him to speed up the dispatch of her documents to Alibaugh once the signature is done. Vivek assures the same, but still it takes another two weeks before he does it.

Scrutiny at the Collector office is finally completed. Despite the No objection certificates from all relevant departments and the rest of all documents intact, the Collector's office takes few weeks before the permission is granted.

The Musk in You

Here she is!

This day of early monsoon she is sitting on the extension of one of the windows of her bungalow gazing at her old 1BHK house which no longer belongs to her.

The past few years are lost in unfruitful follow-ups, dealing with unfaithful colleagues, and trying to manage finances and business. It is not only Manav, Rakesh, Mohan and few customers whom they thought would never leave their back; turned their backs.

A child invents the cartwheel with the help of a punctured tyre and an iron rod from the debris and enjoys the happiness of inventing it. This happiness is far more satisfying than all these years of work, sales, and targets to achieve so-called success.

A girl whose nuclear science paper was displayed once on a notice board for the way she used to attempt it and present it landed up doing sales and accounts for her business. That was how her dreams too transformed. In this process, one who used to dream of visiting the house of 'Irving Kaplan' witnessed the nightmares about losing her house.

Money should not become a must to survive; it

should just be a basic need that was what she always thought. But who knows, what destiny is, and probably destiny is all about this. Taking you to where you are destined to be. Landing you in front of challenges and landing you in front of solutions too. It is all about one's perspective.

Kasturi has gone through the roller coaster that life offered.. Complained sometimes, sometimes accepted but never ran away from the problems. She faced them and tried to pass through. Though things were moving but at a very slow pace testing her patience to the extreme.

This is a time when she is not able to identify herself. Follow-ups at the Government offices start taking a toll on her peace of mind. What her daily routine is made up of is not pleasing her and Job satisfaction is at bay. She is missing her work, and her colleagues and feels to be standing in the wrong place altogether. All the decisions she took with a strong state of mind look wrong to her. She feels hopeless, helpless, and unmotivated. Things are improving but she is not able to feel even happy or satisfied.

The bank guarantee provision and profit from Avinash's Cairo project is going to help them with the shifting from outright cash purchase to credit and in no time they can withdraw the amount and return it to Mrs.Agarwal. That obligation is to get over and with the Taurus Medicare dealership, there is not going to be much pinch in finances. Taking business forward from this point again is not expected to be difficult. Things are almost under control and it is just a matter of time now. Maybe a month or two!

Like sand flows slowly out of a fist her problems too are slowly flowing out now but very slowly indeed. All this exercise for years now is only helping her coach to be on track but that is not enough for her. All those who trusted her are also struggling to streamline their lives. She feels greater responsibility towards them.

By this time Kasturi is tired mentally, physically, and psychologically. Unfortunately, she loses interest in one and all matters by now. It is a feeling like a complete year has passed attending classes and studying hard and trying to understand the subject but, exam is yet to appear, the result is yet to be declared and it is just the day when the exam begins.

She is trying hard to get up early and go back to her earlier routine of work, chants, yoga, her singing, her daily walks, and her most awaited hour with her friends chit-chatting and laughing for silly reasons. But, she lands up getting up and sitting in one place till it is high time to get up for the day. Many times she tries hard and sits to chant but nothing flows, everything appears to be standstill to her. Her eyes appear closed and her face calm but her mind full of all entangled emotions. She fails to focus on her true self. Rather she fails to find her true self. She fails to understand if it is the end of her problems or the beginning of further challenges?

It seems to be a long and tiring journey. Every time

she closes her eyes she recollects how her siblings would all lie down on the bed and Kasturi would sing for them until they sleep. Kasturi wants to go back to those days. But that's really out of reach now. She feels her body to be like a particle randomly and aimlessly wandering in the universe. She feels that something wants to come out of her physical body. Throughout the day and through the night she starts feeling this pull. Nights are just for lying down and days managing heavy eyelids. This all scares her like never before. She understands that she needs help, desperately but is not aware who that help would be.

Kasturi decides to take professional help and approaches a Psychologist sourced through the internet. The first session just concludes her condition of depression and that she will require being even on antidepressants for a few months. Mild sedative enables her to fall asleep at night but carries after-effects throughout the day. It doesn't take long for her to understand that the medications are not helping. The nauseatic feeling throughout the day adds to her irritation. Waiting for Avinash's return from Cairo seems endless.

Kasturi starts avoiding going to the office and making calls as well. With difficulty, she manages to cook and the rest of the day is spent lying on the couch with her laptop ON. She fails to understand why she is breaking down yet again when things are moving on the right side of the origin. All these years she stood strong but falling weak now? Why?

She is shocked when both her kids come to her, Varun holds her hand while Akshay says "you never give us medicine when we are sick and give us only healthy food and tell us that body will take care and heal itself." Varun utters in-between "Now why are you taking medicines? Then you sleep before putting me to sleep, I don't like that."

This is more than enough for her to abruptly discontinue medicines. This results in more and more discomfort, mood swings, and hot flushes, courtesy menopausal period as well. All this becomes too much for her to manage. It also starts taking a toll on her kids who are not able to understand the unusual anger of their sweet mom.

Tonight she refuses to lie down. When sleep fails to accompany her she gets up, it is 3.30 am. She slowly walks to her terrace with half-open eyes. The breeze is warm even at this hour. She looks up at the sky and the moon smiles at her. Her heavy eyes sight the distant moon whose light scatters as she tries to open her eyes further. She recollects how it felt to see the moon while she was young. A fade sketch on the moon is witnessed by her and no one else. There is a face right there, sweet and chubby with deep dimples on both cheeks, dry but hopeful eyes, a big circled vermilion on the forehead, and grey hairs peeking out of her saree pallu covering her head. Pleasant face smiles at Kasturi, it looks radiant and focused on her. Kasturi is no longer in her senses. She wants to reach up there and embrace that face. She keeps on staring and sits down where she is. Closing her eyes, she still tries to visualise the view for long and long.

The moon disappears and tiny Kasturi hugs her grandmother tightly trying to make her arms meet each other but fails to do so. She pats the big fat tummy of her grandma saying "this is my tabla" and jumps and laughs. Her grandma holds both her hands together and kisses them. Looks deep into Kasturi's eyes, "Yes darling, it is your table, play it. Play it yourself and sing and dance to your tune, in your way. Don't try to find peace in the materialistic world; it is just the ambiance for your being. Your peace is inside you. You know that always. Just recollect it yourself. Identify the fragrance of your musk which is within you and let it be carried by the breeze all around you, through the rains and the springs, through the rivers and the mountains, through the happiness and the sorrow as well. Life is all about never-ending challenges. Do not fear them, Play them. Grandma holds Kasturi's both hands together, kiss them again. Her eyes shine and the shine penetrates deep into Katuri's heart. Kasturi inhales sharply as her hands suddenly feel empty. She joins them, holds them close to her heart, and weeps silently for a while.

The whole of the next day Grandma occupies her thoughts. Grandma's words penetrate deep into her heart, her mind, and her soul. Throughout the day she scribbles several times on her writing pad and writes on her palm as well in bold 'The Musk in you'. She feels something deep down. She gets the feeling of realizing something but what? It is not known to her yet.

Consecutive nights she gets up around the same time not knowing why and how? Meditation is far from reach yet. Brahma muhurta would be good as said by experts but for Kasturi, it turns out to be those extra hours where she could do any such things which she is not able to do throughout the day. She decides to pen down that entire she faced in past years and utilizes these holy hours to satisfy the urge from within and feel better than ever throughout the day.

Katuri writes and decides to publish once again and spread her essence and wishes that everyone who reads finds their Musk. They too understand that problems come to make you understand what is within you. Your strength, your ability, your true self which already exists, exists for you to discover.

It is not important where she begins or where she will end. What is important is the journey of how she sailed through, how she passed through. The destination may be beautiful of course but what is remarkable and enjoyable is the journey and the realization that 'Musk is in you' and not in the outer world.

Kasturi eventually finds her rhythm to dance in the rain rather than waiting for the storm to pass.

It is the weekend; Kasturi opens her eyes which are less stressed today. She is not bothered about the time she got up, any chants or prayers.Any rituals are not meant for achieving any wishes today. She feels calm and serene. She is aware she is still not back to her yoga and her singing and many more things she wants to do but that is ok with her for now. She is going to give herself some time and that too will be back and part of her routine soon, she feels. She lifts her phone and an e-mail notification flashes.

Dear Madam,

"Referring to your email

Want to request your time on a phone call today/Monday to understand this proposal better. Please suggest a suitable time for discussion with you."

And The New Beginning............

Challenges or accomplishments, all Welcomed!!

One afternoon as Kasturi's grandma rests, tiny Kasturi runs towards her and jumps and sits on her tummy requesting her to tell her story of the infant Krishna wrongly accused of eating a bit of dirt, which she listens several times with the same passion. Kasturi's eye shine grasping the lesson in the story and her smile depicts far deep understanding as she listens to her grandma's soft voice "Yashodha comes up to him and scolds him "you should not eat dirt" Krishna replies in his very very sweet voice "I haven't." Yashodha orders "Show me, open your mouth" Krishna passes a mischievous smile and opens his mouth. Yashodha gasps looking at what she sees. She sees the entire universe in Krishna's mouth. Yashodha sees all planets, stars, all the land and the sea. She sees all the days and nights, the entire earth and all life in them; she sees the universe until her house in there in its place. She asks Krishna to close his mouth while she is still gasping.

Kasturi claps and laughs and opens her mouth asking her grandma to see if she too can see the Universe in Kasturi's mouth. Grandma laughs saying, "you naughty girl." Kasturi hugs her grandma saying "everyone has universe inside oneself" and she runs away.

Afterword

My debut novel was not planned; it was a compilation of my memories which I penned as and when I felt the urge to write.

Thought of KASTURI arised from looking at the challenges many entrepreneurs face. Facing the financial challenges to coping up with challenges on personal front and also trying to manage all odds in the business simultaneously without giving up is the key to success.

KASTURI is an attempt to acknowledge this struggles and honest efforts.

'KASTURI' comes from my grandma's name 'Kasturabai' who is always alive in my thoughts and this inspires how the protagonist too is attached to her grandmother who makes her find the strength from within. Hence, the title KASTURI 'the musk in you' was instant and profoundly from the bottom of my heart.

I wish 'KASTURI' touches the heart of my readers and help them discover their MUSK.

DOWN THE MEMORY LANE

Author's debut novel 'Down the Memory Lane', 2019
Awardee – Emerging author of the year 2022
Official Critics review - 4/5 stars
Amazon current rating- 4.8/5 stars
Goodread current rating - 4.44/5 stars

This girl, an engineering graduate from Mumbai, shares her experience during the tours she undertook for work purposes. She describes different characters (people) she met and how they became a part of her journey called life.

From some she got some good experience and from some she got to learn. She lives not only with her family and friends but shares her life with the memories of all those who accompanied her during that respective patch of the path she has travelled through. Coming from a lower-middle-class background, the journey was not easy but she sailed through.

She owes her fearless approach and confident personality to all of them. She is a woman of the family who set an example for everyone.

9 789356 803428